MW00834923

Praise

MRS. JOB'S CHOICE

For those grappling with a *new normal,* here's a spirited handbook for the raveled soul. Through vivid scenes from the imagined life of Job's never-named wife, author Linda Jo Reed explores the nature of loss and the art of lament, then and now. Harrowing contemporary stories include a catastrophic mudslide, cancer, an internment camp, family estrangement, births, deaths, brides, and more. Through them all, Reed shows us women of faith who not only survive, but compellingly *live* their deepest questions. How is it that questions help us feel so honestly heard and held?

—Laurie Klein, author of *Where the Sky Opens* and the classic chorus "I Love You, Lord"

"The Lord gave. And the Lord has taken away. And the Lord restored." Linda Jo's capture of Mrs. Job's life—on this side of the veil—encourages my heart. When I recall to mind that our Lord not only allows demolition, but oversees the priceless reconstruction, I take heart once again. *Mrs. Job* holds up a mirror to the human condition with which we are so familiar when God gives —and when He takes away. It is in those seasons, however long they may linger, that "His mercy is showcased in our lives as it was in the lives of Job and his wife," as Linda Jo so eloquently stated.

Each woman's story, including her own, shared within these pages, is a showcase of the Lord's mercy and covenant commitment to bring about His righteous conclusion. Well I know, as one in a multitude of others, that *weeping may endure for the night, but joy comes in the morning!* Linda Jo's storytelling against the backdrop of events in *Mrs. Job* is, in turn, a showcase of the Lord's majesty wrapped in His unfailing love for extremely human hearts and lives. How heartening to see with eyes of faith, His pen poised over the books of our lives: "And the Lord . . ." Faithful. True. Father of good gifts to His children.

—Nancy Bentz / Mrs. Shammah
Shammahs Field LLC & Shammah Ministries

If you're looking for stories of raw pain that produce courage and Spirit-led inspiration, or uniquely vulnerable stories to uplift your journey, you've found it in *Mrs. Job's Choice*. Poignant stories of real people are found in "plot twists" in their books of life. Meditation and journal questions found in every chapter are fresh and practical. Delightful, vulnerable prayers go deep, and they invite growth found in intimate times with the Lord. If a time of irrational pain has discouraged you, this exceptional book invites you to fresh encounters with a trustworthy God.

—Lynn Hare, award-winning author, trainer, coach
Author of *The Quest for Self-Forgiveness*

Linda Jo opens the door for the reader to venture in finding the one true way to our Father in heaven so He can hold us in His arms while going through despair and heartache. She shows how God gives us peace and comfort. This book is a very good read, and I highly recommend it.

—Sandra Lee Cleary, author of *The Stranger in the Polka Dot Tie* and *White Moccasins*

MRS. JOB'S
CHOICE

MRS. JOB'S CHOICE

A Journey of Encouragement

LINDA JO REED

Foreword by Angela Breidenbach

REDEMPTION PRESS

© 2020 by Linda Jo Reed. All rights reserved.

Published by Redemption Press, PO Box 427, Enumclaw, WA 98022.

Toll-Free (844) 2REDEEM (273-3336)

Redemption Press is honored to present this title in partnership with the author. The views expressed or implied in this work are those of the author. Redemption Press provides our imprint seal representing design excellence, creative content, and high-quality production.

No part of this publication may be reproduced, stored in a retrieval system, or transmitted in any way by any means—electronic, mechanical, photocopy, recording, or otherwise—without the prior permission of the copyright holder, except as provided by US copyright law.

Unless otherwise indicated, all Scripture quotations are taken from the New King James Version (NKJV). Copyright © 1982 by Thomas Nelson, Inc. Used by permission. All rights reserved.

Scripture quotations marked NIV are taken from the Holy Bible, New International Version®, NIV®. Copyright ©1973, 1978, 1984, 2011 by Biblica, Inc.® Used by permission. All rights reserved worldwide.

Scripture quotations marked MSG are taken from The Message, copyright © 1993, 2002, 2018 by Eugene H. Peterson. Used by permission of NavPress. All rights reserved. Represented by Tyndale House Publishers, Inc.

Scripture quotations marked ESV are taken from the ESV® Bible (The Holy Bible, English Standard Version®), copyright © 2001 by Crossway, a publishing ministry of Good News Publishers. Used by permission. All rights reserved.

Scripture quotations marked NASB are taken from the New American Standard Bible® (NASB), Copyright © 1960, 1962, 1963, 1968, 1971, 1972, 1973, 1975, 1977, 1995 by The Lockman Foundation. Used by permission. www.Lockman.org

Permissions granted by all individuals whose stories are recorded in this book, 2020.

Edited by Rebecca Florence Miller, freelance writer/editor, rmiller001@luthersem.edu

Portions of the book are fictional.

The Mrs. Job vignettes at the beginning of each chapter are exercises in imaginative biblical storytelling.

ISBN: 978-1-64645-195-1 (Paperback)
978-1-64645-196-8 (ePub)
978-1-64645-197-5 (Mobi)

Library of Congress Catalog Card Number: 2020910670

DEDICATION

To all the lovely ladies who allowed me to tell your stories: Patty, Sandy, Diane, Jane, Fran, Gena, Janet, Marie, Brenda, Gail, Karen, Connie, Gerry, Guyla, Lucille, Cathy, Debbie, and Jeanne.

I tread on holy ground, and I am humbled by your trust.

CONTENTS

Acknowledgments xi

Foreword by Angela Breidenbach xiii

Preface xv

Chapter One: Loss and Disorientation 21

Chapter Two: Stress and Abandonment 41

Chapter Three: Repentance and Forgiveness 67

Chapter Four: Acceptance and Compassion 93

Chapter Five: Silence and Listening 121

Chapter Six: Belief and Trust 151

Afterword 175

About the Author 179

Endnotes 181

ACKNOWLEDGMENTS

As is true with the creation of books, many hands touched and many eyes looked over this manuscript. It seems that I am not the only person who has wondered what happened to Mrs. Job after her famous outburst.

I want to thank all the women who allowed me to interview them and write their stories. I hope I have done justice and honor to all of you. You are great women of faith! I am amazed at God's workmanship in your lives.

The Scribettes, my writing group, have encouraged me since the idea first occurred to me to do more about Mrs. Job than speculate. Thank you, Gail, Dianna, Diane, Karena, and Joann. I am so grateful for your support.

Thank you to my friends Gail, Connie, and Jeanne who read my manuscript to catch those pesky grammar and spelling mistakes. Your insights gave me great ideas, too. I'm sure I couldn't have finished this project without your input.

Thank you, Rebecca Miller, for editing this manuscript. Your suggestions kept me rewriting and made this book a much better work because of your dedication. I appreciate you! Any lingering mistakes are mine.

Thank you, Angela Breidenbach, for writing a foreword for me. Your kindness and help, even through your busy schedule, blessed me so much.

I appreciate your graciousness, Athena Dean Holtz, when you accepted my manuscript at Redemption Press. It was good to talk with you again after a long time, and I stand by what I said—that I trust you with my precious words.

Carrie Stevenson, thank you for stepping in to be my Project Manager, even through such a difficult time in isolation from Covid-19. I value the work you did that moved *Mrs. Job* along in the publishing process.

Thank you, Dori Harrell, for patience while working with my manuscript.

Thank you, Nate Myers, for the fabulous cover. If my book is judged by its cover, everyone will pick it up.

Above all, thank You, Jesus, my Lord and Savior, for Your guiding hand. I am blessed.

FOREWORD

Oh, Mrs. Job, I don't like you. But then I think that means I don't like me. You're much more like me than I want to admit. Too much. My litany may have different words, but we sing the same tune. We've shaken our fists at Father God completely unseeing of His reasons.

You become surprisingly sympathetic as I read about your loss, grief, and anger. Though you lash out verbally at your husband, I don't think you're any different than someone who has questioned the goodness of God against severe pain and problems. Here in the pages of this book, God meets us both and helps us to understand that He is much bigger than we can imagine. He can shoulder the overwhelming emotions we don't understand. We will not put Him off by our lack of understanding.

Mrs. Job, I'm so glad to have met you today. You've helped me to see God loves me even when I'm hurting.

—Angela Breidenbach, Christian Authors Network president and best-selling author

PREFACE

I wince every time I hear a comment about "the wicked Mrs. Job." Who of us hasn't shaken a fist at God when our world has crashed around us? I have been a believer in Jesus for a long time. In my first book, *Upheld in the Battle*, I chronicled my walk of faith. My husband suffered through physical and mental anguish, and for thirty years I travailed his path with him. My own corresponding distress caused me to spiritually shake my fist at God more than once. Instead of being hit by a lightning bolt, I learned of God's faithfulness, patience, and love.

I have noticed most of us have the same kind of reaction Mrs. Job displayed when we protest God allowing a terrible circumstance in our lives. Perhaps we moderate our words, but the spirit of them remains.

In minutes, Mrs. Job lost all of her ten children to death. She must have cried out in despair. The next moments brought her losses of home, servants, financial stability, community, social standing, lifestyle, and finally, the loss of her husband's very health. She must have been terrified for her future.

If this sounds bizarre, think about how long it takes for a tornado to do complete destruction. Or a hurricane? Earthquake? Fire? Mudslide? Or any other disaster. How would your faith and mine hold up under such pressure?

As days followed days, while Mrs. Job adjusted to becoming a homeless object of pity, Job's terrible agonies began. She snapped and cried out her famous and only recorded words: "Do you still hold fast to your integrity? Curse God and die!" (Job 2:9).

We recoil at this and shake our heads at her. But what about our own responses when personal disasters press us? How do we respond to one who has lost everything, including hope? We can judge and condemn, or we can react with empathy. After all, one day it could be us who needs help and understanding.

Mrs. Job was overwhelmed. Who wouldn't be? As I looked closer at her, I saw a woman who suffered greatly—as we all do when unexpected disaster comes upon us. I believe Mrs. Job can teach us how to live through catastrophe and despair and come out trusting God on the other side.

At the end of Job's story, God carefully listed what He had restored to Job: double what he had before the adversities overtook him. God even named Job's daughters and gave them equal inheritances with his seven sons—not dowries that would pass into the hands of their eventual husbands. Bestowing an inheritance upon a daughter that would be hers to control would be an unusual action for a father to take. Such was Job's gratitude to God.

With so much detail, I observed one factor that was *not* there. God did not list for us a new wife for Job at the end of his written story. I believe God must have had compassion on this poor woman, given her an opportunity to repent, and then rewarded her for her trusting growth before Him.

I believe God gave Mrs. Job a second chance. He does it for all of us.

Everything we need to live a full life is given to us in the Bible.

Because of it, we discover that God offered His Son to save us from our sins and give us eternal life. I have heard it described as our instruction manual, provided by our manufacturer. If we study it, we receive teachings and guidelines. We learn from those who have gone before us. We see their mistakes and successes. In this manner, God equips us to handle anything.

"All Scripture is given by inspiration of God, and is profitable for doctrine, for reproof, for correction, for instruction in righteousness, that the man of God may be complete, thoroughly equipped for every good work" (2 Timothy 3:16–17).

I hope readers will be encouraged through the stories related here.

God is a great designer and builds great things into His people. I hope this book will show it. I desire that compassion for others would be most important, second chances given and received, then courage and good choices would mark lives lived well. If there is suffering, that it would be endured with patience and grace, to build the character of Jesus.

I have heard of You by the hearing of the ear,
but now my eye sees You.
Job 42:5

ONE

Loss and Disorientation

The Lord gave, and the Lord has taken away;
blessed be the name of the Lord.
Job 1:21

It could have happened this way . . .

Lifting her face for the warm breeze to caress, Mrs. Job hummed. *What a lovely day! Just the kind that makes me feel God is smiling upon me.*

The river irrigation system had made it possible for good crops this year, and her husband's farms had done well. The livestock flourished. Her husband sat in the city gates doing government work, as he did every day when he wasn't checking on farms or animals. At this very moment, their ten children feasted at their eldest son's home. Like Mrs. Job, her friends reveled in the comfort of their lives. Families were cared for, servants supervised and busy, and benevolent duties overseen.

As Mrs. Job plied her needle through the fabric and a delicate embroidery design began to emerge, she pondered that tonight it would be only her and her husband for dinner. Since their ten children were all at her eldest son's home, perhaps she and Job could have a quiet, intimate evening together. She smiled softly.

Job sat at the city gates, an elder who daily judged the affairs of men. Mrs. Job's chest swelled with pride. How fortunate she had been to marry such an influential man! Job was known all over the region for his wisdom, righteousness, and wealth. He could have looked higher for a bride, but he chose her!

And how he loves the children! What father rises early to offer sacrifices for the souls of his children? I am so privileged.

The filmy draperies softly swayed with the gentle wind through the covered terrace where Mrs. Job sat contented. The day was warm, but here she could rest with her cloth and needle and let down her veil. She pushed her fingers through her hair to loosen it slightly.

Right then, Job staggered into the house, looking like a wild man. His clothing was torn. His bare head had been shaven. What was this?

"Husband!" she cried as she dropped the embroidery and ran to him. "What happened?"

Tears poured from his reddened eyes, and he gathered her close. "Oh, my dear," he moaned. "They are gone! Everything is gone! The Lord gave and the Lord has taken away; blessed be the name of the Lord!" His arms cradled her gently, and he rested his chin upon her head as quiet sobs shook his frame.

Alarm stabbed at Mrs. Job's heart. She struggled to lean back and see his face.

"What are you saying? What do you mean? What is gone? What has the Lord taken away?"

A great shudder went through Job, and a sigh came from deep within him.

"Come, sit down." He led her to a bench.

"What?" she demanded.

He took her hands in his. "My dear," he began—and stopped. Again he opened his mouth as if to speak, but then shut it and shook his head.

As she waited, tension built between her shoulder blades. Her back grew stiff as she sat straighter. She stared into his ashen face and saw new lines.

"Today the sun ceases to shine upon us. Messengers have come to me one by one with tales of calamities. The Sabeans raided our livestock and killed our servants. What animals left were burned to death by a mysterious fire from heaven. While he was still speaking, another messenger said the Chaldeans formed bands and stole our camels and goods and killed those servants too. Each escaped alone to tell me." Job released one of her hands to run his own across his eyes and grabbed the edge of his tunic to wipe his face.

Mrs. Job froze in dread. *No. This couldn't have happened—all in one day?*

"Wife," he said as he took her hand in his again, "there is more."

She jumped up and screamed. "No! No, not more!" She covered her face with her hands.

"While our children dined in our eldest son's home today," he hesitated and gulped, "suddenly a great wind came across the four corners of the house and—it fell on them." He wiped his eyes again, then keened, "They were all killed. Only one servant escaped to tell us."

Job stood in time to catch his sobbing wife in his arms.

Meanwhile, in the book of Job . . .

A challenge brought it on. Who would have thought it?

As the biblical story of Job opens, we see God on His throne and the angels around Him. Evidently the devil, the adversary known as Satan, could saunter in and present himself haughtily before God.

"So, where have you come from?" God asks Satan.

I imagine the devil leaning arrogantly against a pillar, with his arms crossed. "I've been wandering around the earth, patrolling."

"Have you seen my servant Job?" God asks, smiling, as He considers this faithful friend on earth. Job trusts God, and that pleases Him. "There is none like him on all the earth, blameless and upright, fearing God and shunning evil."

"Oh yeah, sure," says the devil arrogantly, still propped by the pillar. "You've built this hedge around him, and I can't even get close to him. You let me at him, and he'll curse You to Your face."

God replies to Satan, "All right, then. Go ahead and touch all he has, but do not touch his person."

Picture the speed with which the head demon straightens up, turns with military precision, and marches away to "touch" God's prize. What excitement must drive him to do his dirty work!

This brings us to the day in which the Job couple lost everything. The Scriptures describe Job rising to his feet, tearing his robe, and shaving his head in grief. Then he fell to the ground to worship God.

"Naked I came from my mother's womb," he cried. "And naked I shall return there. The Lord gave, and the Lord has taken away; blessed be the name of the Lord."

And in all this, Job did not sin or charge God with wrong (Job 1:6–12).

Understanding Disorientation and Transition

Loss. It's hard to bear.

How long does it take for disasters like accidents, tornadoes, floods, fires, mudslides, illness, or—death—to happen? In only a moment, life changes forever. Maybe it's a lingering loss, but it brings bewilderment with it.

We plan our lives. We study to enter a career we believe will bring us satisfaction, renown, and success. We start families we hope will make us proud. Then events and our loved ones disappoint us. A life-changing disaster hits us, and we don't know what to do with that.

Perhaps our sorrow becomes a rage that keeps us locked into a place in time. We are hurt, angry, and unable to function as we assimilate what a horrible life circumstance has happened to us. Possibly we are desperate and afraid. How do we deal with perplexing and swirling emotions and questions?

I can relate to Mrs. Job's anger at God in allowing her world to crumble around her. I had always dreamed of living a perfect life. My spouse would be a romantic hero to me and a wise sage to our many obedient children.

My dream crumbled early on when my husband became addicted to prescription drugs, and other mental issues began to surface. At times, I would go off alone just to yell at God. He had known my dreams—why did He allow this kind of life? I lived neglected and rejected. My husband could not support the family in long-term employment, so I became the breadwinner.

Invariably, my anger would burn, and fear stood up front and center. *What will happen to us?* I would wonder. Then I would plot and plan and try to fix everything myself. After all, I had to hold it all together; there was no one else.

I suspect Mrs. Job had no need to grow her spiritual roots very deeply. She was married to a kind man—a pillar of the community, and wealthy. In her culture, she went from her father's house to her husband's house. Maybe she never thought about the trials of others as she planned a sumptuous wedding feast that probably would have included the cream of the society in which she lived.

She led a privileged life. Giving to those not as prosperous as herself might have been ingrained as the right thing for the upper classes to do. She may have given alms to the poor, but perhaps the troubles of the unfortunate did not overly concern her.

She would have set about making a home for a prominent man who sat in the seat of the powerful in the city. She bore him ten children. For a woman, that was a crowning feat. It made her important too. She may have enjoyed her social position, leaving the spiritual development to her husband.

Then the losses struck, and she had no underpinning to sustain her. She may have had no idea what she should do next.

In contrast, though Job did not understand, he decided to trust that God knew why these misfortunes had befallen him. It seemed that God trusted Job to remain a steadfast witness no matter the provocation.

Living with adversity is complicated. Often, we walk stoically through life, putting on a brave front and pretending we don't need anyone's help. When something goes wrong, we fake it, because we think we can handle it. We don't think clearly. If asked, we may deny anything is wrong. Perhaps we fool ourselves by denial. This way, we can go for some time before we trip over the obvious. We might cover our eyes and ears as we sob, like Mrs. Job, or we might cry out our grief before God and move forward into it like Job.

Not every loss or change comes through trauma. Sometimes it's a job switch or a move to a new home or a new neighborhood. It could be something seemingly simple, but it knocks us off our balance, and we are disoriented. Life is not what it was before. We wonder what's next.

As we move into our "new normal," it's okay to be distracted and confused. It is temporary. There is no need to try to operate as usual. Disorientation is a shock absorber for our souls. It cushions us from harsh realities until we are ready to face them. I believe this is one of God's tender mercies to keep us in a safe place until we are ready to move into the next phase of life.

Until then, this is a time to wait. Pastor Rod Cosgrove, at Garland Alliance Church in Spokane, Washington, preached about this one Sunday. He said, "Sometimes life puts us in a crisis where things have unexpectedly changed. Uncertain of what to do next, we often go back to what we've known before—a familiar place, a familiar person, or perhaps to a familiar community. We do this hoping it will maybe make things clearer, that we can figure out what happened and reassess where we stand in the hopes that we will eventually find our way through the unfamiliar place."[1] He went on to caution his hearers not to make hasty decisions in a moment of crisis. It might be best to wait for a while, and then ask God for clarification.

This event that crashed in on us may not be what we expected, but we have God's Word to tell us He is working out a solution for us. Paul wrote, "And we know that all things work together for good to those who love God, to those who are the called according to His purpose" (Romans 8:28). God is shaping us for His purpose, and that takes time.

Disorientation can occur anywhere. All it takes is being out of place or out of our comfort zones. I had an opportunity to go to China some time ago. What an adventure! I was to meet the team I would join once I arrived. After nearly a year of planning and spinning details, I boarded an airplane alone, and with trepidation, for my first trip abroad. What if I missed something? What if I got lost? What if no one met me? What if . . .

I landed safely in Beijing after a twenty-plus-hour airplane ride. The night sky showed through the skylights of the terminal as weary travelers were all herded to customs. Somehow, I found my way through to the baggage carousel, only to discover that my baggage had not arrived with me. Tingles of fear radiated to my fingertips. What should I do? It was nearly midnight, Beijing time. Everywhere I looked, signs were written in Chinese. The people around me spoke Chinese. How would I find help at that time of night? How could I find out about my luggage? The panic mounted and my heart pounded. I could even feel it in my temples.

I had never felt so helpless. I'm a take-charge kind of person, and "helpless" was not in my vocabulary.

I stood alone and isolated. *God, help me! I'm afraid! I can't function in this alien place!* Then I heard in my mind: *Calm down and think. I am here in China too. You are not alone.*

For the next hour, I struggled through the language barrier in the luggage claims office, filling out papers and arranging for the Beijing airport to keep my bag locked up for a week until I could return to claim it. When it arrived the next night, I would be across the country. With those arrangements made, I prayed my greeter would still be waiting for me. I sighed with relief when I saw her. Thank You, Lord.

Our God is with us. He promises to be with us in every circumstance. He is our comfort. When we call upon Him, He rushes to our side to comfort us.

The companion of disorientation is transition. A new normal. Most of us would not choose this way, but we find we have been thrust into it. How long will it last? Is what we feel typical? Can't we simply get over it and go back to what we were doing? Other people around us don't seem to go through this. Sometimes merely coming to the place of making the transition is confusing. What if we get stuck?

Transition is not necessarily a bad thing. Sometimes it's a very good thing. Whichever it is, change is essential. Growth cannot happen without it. When disorientation hits, perhaps we are at a growth point. It could be a signal to change direction.

We realize we can't do what we did before. It doesn't work anymore. We must find new ways of living, of doing things.

Without losses that throw us into change, it's doubtful we would ever find our true potential. The mystery is that through the disorientation and the transition, we find roots of strength in God as He stretches and develops us into the creations He always meant for us to become.

Seth Godin has said that coming and going matter far more than what happens in the middle: "We mistakenly spend most of our time thinking about, working on and measuring the in-between parts, imagining that this is the meat of it, the important work. In fact, humans remember the transitions, because it's moments of change and possibility and trepidation that light us up."[2]

If waiting is good while experiencing disorientation, then what kinds of actions could we take in preparation for transition?

We stop motion.

We listen for His voice.

We draw on Scripture verses we may remember.

We deliberately calm our emotions.

We let Him draw us deeper into trusting Him when everything around us screams panic.

We let companions show us new paths ahead, instead of resisting their wisdom.

Then we move forward.

Living with the Mystery of God

Have you ever wondered what you could observe if the veil were lifted and you could glimpse beyond the here and now? I'm not sure I want to know what's in the future. How about you? What if we don't like it? It's possible we could see our efforts bring success. That would be welcome. It's also possible we might see disasters. Uh-oh.

Certainly, it would be our preference to understand the reasons why, but comprehending may not make events easier or harder to handle.

Only God knows all things. Perhaps that's for the best in the long run of life.

Who would want to know if there is a disaster looming? Then again, maybe we would mishandle successes if we knew what awaited us. Recognizing that God is sovereign allows for us to learn and grow unreservedly, even if we make mistakes.

How often do we take the time to contemplate mystery? It's amazing to think God identifies every star in the sky by name. Every star's exact location. And how long it took for its light to reach our gazes on earth. It's inviting to sit on a quiet beach in the refreshing evening coolness, to contemplate the vastness of the universe as the moon simmers on watery ripples.

"The heavens declare the glory of God . . . day unto day utters speech, and night unto night reveals knowledge" (Psalm 19:1–2).

The sun "rejoices like a strong man to run its race. Its rising is from one end of heaven, and its circuit to the other end; and there is nothing hidden from its heat" (Psalm 19:5–6).

On that same beach, the daytime looks far different. The sunlit, translucent waves roll in on our toes in shades of blue, green, and white. The sky is still vast, but we can't look up without shading our eyes. The heat warms our skin. We can consider the many facets of the sun, described in the Scripture above, as racing across the sky above us. God put it there to sustain life.

But we are mostly in a hurry. We just want to get answers so we can move on. Our schedules demand it. Other times, the *why* is squeezed from our grieving hearts.

It's beyond us to understand the unfathomable depths of God. He is eternal, holy . . . other.

He is indiscernible from a human perspective. His depths are greater than we can plumb, even if we have eternity to try.

Human history is moving toward a culmination that God ordained from the beginning. What looks like chaos to us has an order to it that will be revealed at the right time.

It's okay not to have all knowledge.

But God doesn't leave us without hope. This eternal, holy, unfathomable God knows each one of us inside out. He loves us.

Sandy's Story

At 10:37 on Saturday morning, March 22, 2014, as neighbors went about their usual routines, a massive mudslide changed the Oso community in Washington State forever. Forty-three people were lost that day, and surviving members of those families still grieve.

Sandy lost her brother and his family, the youngest only four years old. Sandy remembers hearing the news Sunday morning while she was at church. She immediately tried to call her brother, but to no avail. As the news unfolded, a surreal horror settled over her.

"I remember those days seemed like slow motion. Waiting for news and watching it on TV and realizing, *This is my family!* It just couldn't be real."

Authorities requested relatives provide identifying marks. Sandy shared her brother's, and then she sat glued to the television as one body and then another were found. A week passed before rescuers uncovered her brother and his stepson.

"That was just like them. They did everything together," Sandy observed. As the news came, her mind fuzzed up and she couldn't quite absorb the truth. *This really happened,* she kept reminding herself.

Sandy, her husband Bill, and her sister Connie traveled to the site, but were not able to view it the first time. Family members were protected from seeing their loved ones extracted from mud and debris. But they did check in with the Red Cross at a staging area. Other organizations were there as well. They talked with FEMA workers.

The disaster disrupted all normal life. Fresh anguish rolled in waves as each family member was found; one here and one there over a period of several weeks.

During the second trip to the Oso site, Sandy and Bill met with FEMA workers, and two Billy Graham Rapid Response Team chaplains went with them to the site.

"My brother and sister-in-law had recently moved there not long before the mudslide. They were excited about their retirement cabin on the river. We hadn't even gone over to see it yet, so I had no point of reference as I looked on the scene," Sandy explained. That, too, was disorienting as she tried to place her family, in her mind, somewhere on the hill before the cataclysm.

The chaplains spent a lot of time with Sandy and Bill, listening. "At that time, it was so good to be with other Christians."

Two or three people were still missing at that point, including Sandy's four-year-old grandnephew. They prayed at the site.

"We tried to be mindful of the presence of Lord," Sandy said. "The chaplains were like a protection around us. When we couldn't function, they would ask the questions for us. We could depend on them to start prayer and take care of things. Everything was a blur."

During the third trip over, Sandy and Bill learned their grand-nephew had finally been found. "This was a blessing; he was our last one. Still, I can't say there was closure—how can there ever be closure? And what does closure mean, anyway?"

A passage of Scripture kept popping up from different sources to give Sandy encouragement: "Blessed be the God and Father of our Lord Jesus Christ, the Father of mercies and God of all comfort, who comforts us in all our tribulation, that we may be able to comfort those who are in any trouble, with the comfort with which we ourselves are comforted by God. For as the sufferings of Christ abound in us, so our consolation also abounds through Christ" (2 Corinthians 1:3–5).

One evening, while Sandy watched TV, she saw a musician

playing music in a bar. He was playing for the Oso victims. When his interviewer asked him why, he said that as part of the community, he needed to help, to give back. So he did what he could: he played music and gave the donations to Oso families.

"I was struck with what he said. I asked myself, 'What can I do?' I thought then, *I can pray.*" A friend, who was herself a Billy Graham Rapid Response Team chaplain, introduced Sandy to the organization, and she went through the training. Since then, Sandy has served with the group in several states after major disasters. She is helping and giving back. She is now asking questions for stunned families who can't think during trauma.

"It's an honor and a privilege to come alongside people, be a presence for them, and listen to their stories. They need the same compassion that we needed in those initial stages of despair. I can pray for them as they grieve."

Through participation in the chaplain program, Sandy can help others in their time of trauma, and she feels the presence of God.

"We have to stay focused and connected with God, or there is no abundant life. Jesus *is* the Abundant Life. I hear Him saying, *The closer you are to Me, the more life and peace you have.*"

God Knows the Whys

Have you considered that the Evil One may consider us as pawns in a challenge too? What an uncomfortable thought! Perhaps mystery is a good idea after all.

The truth is that human beings *are* hostages in a cosmic struggle. In the beginning, the Scriptures tell us, God made a perfect man and woman and placed them in a perfect world setting—a garden where they would lack nothing.

The adversary, the devil, then attempted to thwart God's perfect plan. He tempted the human beings who followed Him. Their fall from grace as they agreed with the devil resulted in a curse on all humankind. But God made a provision in sending His Son, Jesus, to die on a cross to redeem us back to God. In His resurrection, Jesus once again opened a way for us to live with God forever in a perfect relationship. It's our choice, then, to be set free by the sacrifice of Jesus or to live in the bondage of the curse.

Salvation is being worked out on the earth until God's predetermined time frame. Through the instructions given to us in the Bible, we do spiritual warfare in an unseen arena.

We must be on our knees before God in prayer because we have an Enemy after our souls—one who wants us to ignore God and lead a self-absorbed life without Him.

I certainly don't want to be a pawn. I intend to stand strong with roots into the Spirit of God. How about you?

Another nugget of wisdom Pastor Rod passed on to us was this:

> Don't lose heart.
> It may seem like little is happening, or that the right thing isn't happening, but that's not entirely true.
> God has plans for our lives. It's true that He brings wonderful good out of the bad things that happen.[3]

Hope is possible once we can leave the whys in God's hands. There is a freedom to move forward. In his book *The Healing Path,* Dan Allender said, "Hope is not naïve desire but a calculated risk that declares, whatever the loss, it is better than remaining where we were."[4]

What a relief to grasp that we are not alone in our catastrophes. God is always present with us and understands every blow that falls. His compassion is ceaseless, and His mercies are new for us every morning. He is closer than a cry away.

He works in places we don't see. While we may show a masked face to the world, God works in those depths we don't reveal to anyone—including ourselves! He follows His own plan, and the results benefit everyone involved—even if it doesn't look so very good to us at the time.

It's not up to us to fix it.

Our part is to wait on answers in God's time.

To trust He will accomplish His purposes.

Precisely as He designs.

And pray.

Patty's Story

Touched as several friends experienced breast cancer, Patty felt God's call to do what she could to support them. She would listen, drive them to appointments, and make herself available as needed. She opened her home to her friend Diana, and for a year Patty served her until Diana passed away.

Then came the dreaded diagnosis—now applied to Patty. At first, shock overwhelmed her. After helping friends, Patty herself had contracted breast cancer. She knew only too well what could lie ahead. Rather than bringing life to a halt, Patty wanted to rush into "fixing it" as quickly as possible and get it behind her. "I wondered how this was going to affect me. Would people treat me differently?"

"I'll be there for you," her son, Johnny, assured her; she would not be alone. Patty's friends who had gone before her and survived also rallied around her. This brought Patty to the place of transition.

With all the support, medical wisdom, and a game plan, Patty said, "I know God's got it!"

From the beginning, Patty says it was no accident she had always been called to support her friends in their fight against breast cancer. God knew she would need this experience. Patty's trust in God continued to grow as she moved through treatment.

Patty has moved into recovery. "I asked the 'Why me?' question at first. But now I see. It's important to connect with people when you go through something like this. As I look back, I can see how God orchestrated everything to this point."

She is thankful to be cancer-free and blessed that she didn't have to go through chemo or radiation.

Patty leads a Life Group for her church. Her ladies thank her for her ministry of prayer among them. Mirroring the Old Testament prophet Samuel, Patty tries to hear what God says daily. She invites Him, "Speak, Lord; Your servant is listening."

"Something happens every day. God gives me opportunities to listen, then to go and do."

There are different ways to hear from God—possibly as many ways as there are people. God created us in His image. Patty quoted her pastor: "What does God sound like? Why, He often sounds like you!" His voice is easily recognizable by each person. He talks to us in ways that are already familiar to us.

God will always meet us at our point of need. He brings us confidence that He will never leave us nor forsake us, no matter how desperate our situation appears to us. He is present with us and always ready with hope, and He will be there on the other side of our trauma waiting for us. The light is ahead. We only need to keep walking forward.

Dealing with It

Life is not forever on this earth. We are left asking, "How am I going to deal with it?"

We have several options.

We can throw temper tantrums. Does it help? No. Does it make us feel better? No. Does it make the problem go away? No.

We can try to control our outcomes. But disasters will come along, and often they are not controllable by human beings.

There is a place for grieving, but don't wallow too long. Your spirit needs joy to balance grief for survival.

We can face it. Accept the reality. Maybe it will go away; maybe it won't. But if we mean to move forward in life, we must face those things we dislike or fear. We must deal with it.

We can go to our knees and surrender our lives to God. He is the only One with answers. He loves us like no other. He has the plan for our lives.

God's Plan

When we have surrendered our lives to God, we surrender our right to ourselves. We join His family. We join His team. He has a plan that He is busy working out for—big picture—His creation, humankind. We are part of that plan. We are not autonomous. Each of us is a strand woven into God's big-picture plan.

Bad things that happen aren't what God would want, because He is all good. Before the fall of man in the garden of Eden, God had a very different plan for us—one with love, companionship, and walking with Him in the cool of the day, face to face with Him. But with rebellion came disease and disasters.

The devil is *still* stomping around trying to steal from us, kill us, and destroy us.

In spite of the devil's tantrums, God's plans remain. He can use the catastrophes of our lives to bring about the changes in us to prepare us for the glorious eternity that is yet to come.

After the great flood disaster in which Noah obeyed God and built an ark, God placed a rainbow in the sky as a symbol of His assurance that He would not destroy humankind with a global flood again. After it rains, look at the rainbows arching the sky and remember that God's promises to us are true.

Yes, Dealing with It

Remember God loves us so much, He sent Jesus to give us eternal life.

He carefully plans for each one of us, even when we don't understand His strategy. We are His design and not our own.

Take each day as it comes with thanksgiving.

Take encouragement from reading His Word.

Reach out to community.

Accept help from community.

Trust Him with everything (even the ugly days!).

Believe God. It's our decision. Every time.

> May the God of hope fill you with all joy and peace as you trust in him. (Romans 15:13 NIV)

Meditation Questions

1. Can you relate to Mrs. Job's shallow spiritual roots? What will you do about it?
2. How do you cope when life changes overnight and leaves you with a new reality?
3. How have you reacted when panic overwhelmed you in a situation?
4. In your changing circumstances, what would it take for you to be able to say, like Job did, "The Lord gives, and the Lord takes away; blessed be the name of the Lord"?
5. What does it take for you to "turn the corner" and move on in the face of change or tragedy?
6. Would you be willing to let God use your circumstances to lead you into a new focus for your life?

Journal Question

Can you think of a time when you suffered through disorientation and transition? What did you learn about yourself? What did you learn about God? Take time to write it down and ponder.

Prayer

"The Lord gave, and the Lord has taken away; blessed be the name of the Lord" (Job 1:21).

Lord, our hearts are stunned by the losses we have endured. It makes no sense to us. We wonder how we will recover from the devastation. We have fallen to our knees with the despair of it all. We bring our hearts before You. Only You can hold us up.

TWO

Stress and Abandonment

*And he took for himself a potsherd with which to scrape
himself while he sat in the midst of the ashes.*
Job 2:8

It could have happened this way . . .

Mrs. Job stared with horror, her hand covering her mouth and her eyes filling, as her husband picked up a piece of broken, jagged pottery to scratch the awful sores that were now multiplying on his body daily. She hardly recognized his handsome face anymore, so marred as it was by sores.

The shadows silhouetted his form as he squatted in the opening of the cell where they now dwelled. They lived along the shadows of the city walls. Mrs. Job pushed her damp hair off her forehead. It was so hot! Her old house, also constructed of bricks, had stood close on the side of the ziggurat. All the best families lived up high in the city. How she missed the covered terrace and the filmy draperies that had been so cooling!

The ziggurat stood in the distance, and without its shade, the heat was unbearable. Some other merchant family had taken over her old home since they'd lost everything and could no longer afford to live there. Another thing to raise her ire.

And now, after all the other horrors she'd endured, Mrs. Job had to watch her husband's body waste away as his health deteriorated. It was too much!

Mrs. Job turned from her husband, trembling, and picked up a broom. She glared at the object. Others had always done this job for her, and now she had to do it for herself. She put the broom into motion, sweeping furiously.

No matter how many times I sweep this dirt floor, it never feels clean! Oh, I wish we had a floor covering or a rug! It would help so much.

Despite taking in mending for others, all she could manage was necessities. *At least I learned something useful while growing up. Everyone always praised my stitching.* This caused fresh tears as she remembered that Job sat in the ashes and dirt by the cook fire, unable to help with their living these days. He no longer sat by the gate of the city. Others meted out justice. No one wanted Job around—or her.

Perhaps in the future, she could shop in the market square for some wealthy family to add to her income, but not for a family she had known socially in her past! She did not want to be pitied. She could do that for herself. She shoved the broom, stirring up the dust.

Self-pity had become her constant companion. Pictures flashed across her mind of the commiserating looks from her former friends before they hurried by her. How self-righteous they were! She, Mrs. Job, was now the recipient of charity, where once she had dispensed it. She would never look at "the poor" again in the same way.

My babies! She stopped, put her hands on the end of the broom, and rested her chin on them. Painful memories of chubby cheeks, first teeth, boys chasing each other, and girls learning to stitch under Mrs. Job's expert tutelage caused her to discreetly hit the wall with her broom, glancing at her pitiful husband as she did so. She tried so hard to keep quiet about her feelings out of respect for his.

God, how could You? How could You allow this? What did we ever do to You? My husband has always been faithful to You and kind to people. He has judged fairly at the gate. He doesn't deserve this—and neither do I!

Job groaned and shifted his position.

She couldn't hold it together any longer. Mrs. Job threw down the broom, raised a fist in the air, and yelled, "Do you still hold to your integrity? Curse God and die!"

Both froze. She held her breath. Job looked up into her eyes. The compassion in his eyes belied the firmness of his voice.

"You speak as one of the foolish women speaks. Shall we indeed accept good from God, and shall we not accept adversity?" (Job 2:8–10). He looked at the potsherd in his hand and deliberately scratched his other arm.

Mrs. Job's eyes bulged. She pulled her stare from her husband and fixed it instead on her lowering fist.

Meanwhile, in the book of Job . . .

Before Mrs. Job lost her temper before her beleaguered husband, the adversary had again challenged Job's integrity in the presence of God.

It was another day in heaven, and the angels came to present themselves before God, bowing low before the throne. Rainbows of color swirled around it, and clouds, thunder, and lightning surrounded the enthroned figure. God displayed His magnificence.

As before, the devil, the adversary, sauntered in with confidence in his bearing. Not bowing or giving any deference, he sat haughtily with his arms crossed.

"Where do you come from?" asked God, though He already knew.

"I've been wandering around the earth watching your humans." There may have been some impatience in the answer.

"Have you considered My servant, Job, that there is none like him on the earth, a blameless and upright man, one who fears God and shuns evil? And still he holds fast to his integrity, although you incited Me against him to destroy him without cause." God gave His servant Job a verbal accolade.

Satan jumped to his feet and snorted. "Skin for skin! Yes, all that a man has he will give for his life. But stretch out Your hand now and touch his bone and his flesh, and he will surely curse You to Your face!"

Maybe God studied our adversary, considering the test He would be allowing for His servant Job. At last He spoke: "Behold, he is in your hand, but spare his life" (Job 2:1–7).

Immediately, the devil rushed out of the presence of God to strike Job with another disaster.

Fist Shaking

As if it were not enough that Satan had taken away all of Job's possessions, his children, and his wealth, now he attacked Job's health. It appears that in this contest, Satan was quite confident Job would curse God. How surprised he must have been when it was Mrs. Job who cursed God instead. He must have been very interested in how this would play out on earth.

Mrs. Job, not as composed as her husband, voiced her anger and possibly flung a fist in the air. Her only utterance in the Bible is well-documented. She did not set a stellar example for those who would come after her. Many sermons have quoted her and judged her guilty—of slapping a man when he's already down, of cursing God in her own words—guilty of sin.

Let's consider her aggravations. Stunned by her losses, she lashed out. What mother who has lost ten children at once would not react? In the same moment Mrs. Job lost her children, she lost her home, her servants, her financial standing, her community, and her social standing. All of these encompassed her entire lifestyle. Her husband even lost his health. Her faith was tried and found wanting. She became an object of pity.

How many of us have shaken our fists at God when we have been overwhelmed or disappointed by tragic losses? Our fist shaking might not be as public as hers, but God still sees it.

We lose jobs and marriages; we change churches, and therefore lose friends. We move far and wide seeking jobs, and again we lose friends and family. Loved ones die and leave us hurting. Major illnesses change the courses of our lives. Some of us become caretakers. Perhaps we suffer major financial losses that change our lifestyle dramatically. Lastly, to be the object of anyone's pity rips at our pride.

Where is God? Do we continue to shake our fists at Him and demand answers? We might not utter Mrs. Job's words, but what about our own cries of "God, what do You think You are doing?" "How could You allow this to happen?" "What are You going to do about it?" We walk away from God in our disappointment, thinking He is not worthy of our trust or faith. Isn't that the same thing that made Mrs. Job guilty?

Perhaps we are back to the mystery of God. It's not pleasant to think we could be chess pieces being moved around on a cosmic chessboard. However, the truth is that back in the beginning—in the garden of Eden—humankind handed over earthly authority to the devil. We live with the consequences of the original sin and rebellion against God that our first parents chose.

That does not make it any easier when we suffer, but it does make our fist shaking more understandable.

Abandonment

Once we allow our anger to overcome us and determine God's unworthiness to handle our well-being, the despair of feeling abandoned becomes our companion. What is this state of being? Once we enter it, why is it so frightening? Not that we would admit to fear, because we often identify it as anger.

Parents are supposed to protect and care for their children. But sometimes they live in addictions, or they give their lives over to their own advancement, or they die—and their children are left alone. If God is our Father, then why doesn't He protect us from these painful circumstances?

Governments are supposed to protect and care for their people. But often, leaders are more interested in power, and the people starve. Or another entity comes in to destroy them, and the people flee.

Abandoned. Where is God? Abandonment leaves us to our own inadequate devices.

But where does continuing anger and blame of God lead? Our physical health may suffer. Feelings of worthlessness or of being undervalued, ignored, and unloved all may attack our souls. But if we can look beyond our sense of abandonment, we might see that God is big enough to take our pain. He stands with us in it. This is true, even when we don't have the feelings to believe it. He will give us trail markers along the way to show us that He is always with us and that His plans for us never fail.

After my husband passed away, I sold my house to build a new one. I desperately needed a new start to life. In making the change, I suffered through several setbacks. A flood in the basement was major. It happened the day before a real estate tour planned to introduce my house to selling agents. During this period, a housing mold scare swept the nation. Because of that, I believed my house was blackballed.

Of course, I needed the funds from the old dwelling to build the new house. I watched other homes on my block sell, but mine did not. Some of them were more expensive, and some of them were put up for sale *after* mine. I wrangled with anger. I had to remind myself constantly that God was in this move and He would make it happen, no matter the circumstances around me. Eventually, the house did sell, and in time for the financial deadlines for the new house.

God has not changed. He is our place of safety when the world whirls around us. He is strong. He understands our grief. He always knows what we need. He is faithful. He is trustworthy. He goes before us. He is our rear guard. His arms are around us. His peace is always offered as we trust Him in our storms.

My daughter had a cat named Clyde, and he lived with us from birth until he died at the ripe old age of sixteen. Toward the end of his life, his eyesight was failing, and I suspect his hearing was going as well.

Clyde would sit in midpoint of the hallway in the middle of the night and loudly yowl the way only a Siamese cat can. If any of us hollered at him to be quiet, we were ignored. However, if my daughter yelled at him, he immediately stopped the racket and trotted into her room to snuggle in for the night. I think Clyde wanted to know he was not alone, and then he wanted to know "his person" was present. Then he could be content and unafraid.

I have thought of Clyde in the years since and pondered his wee-hour cries. There have been times I've felt alone, and Clyde would come to mind. Clyde's person always answered him in those dark nights. His person was the only one who could give him comfort.

This illustrates the truth that God is always present with us. He's closer than a brother, closer than we can imagine. He has assured us, repeatedly, that He will never leave us nor forsake us (Hebrews 13:5). He said those who belong to Him cannot be snatched out of His hand (John 10:28). His Word, the Bible, says so—in red-letter words. Jesus Himself gave those assurances. What else do we need to be content?

Our person is there for us.

In the middle of the night, when I call on His name, I am reassured. I can go to sleep.

"He who keeps you will not slumber. Behold, He who keeps Israel shall neither slumber nor sleep. The Lord is your keeper" (Psalm 121:3–5).

Gena's Story

Jack and Gena were set. The plans for their dream European vacation had taken a year to finalize, but were now were in place. For six weeks, they would tour and visit family. Hotels were reserved, plane tickets purchased, and bags packed.

Friends were lined up to care for home, hearth, and animals. In four days, they would board their plane. They couldn't wait!

At the last minute, with everything done, the sun beckoned, and they decided to take a bike ride. Gena knew she was pushing it, but the exercise would do her good.

As they rolled down the street, they heard an engine revving behind them. Someone wanted their space, and fast. Jack went to one side of the street. As Gena steered to the other side, she wished that Jack had installed the mirror on her handlebars that she'd asked for so she could see the roaring car she heard bearing down upon her.

Trying to get out of the way fast, she hit the curb as she went around a corner, and she crashed.

"I knew immediately something was broken." How could it be

otherwise? She heard the crack in her knee, and her back muscles went into spasms.

At the hospital, Gena's doctor told her it was the worst possible break she could endure. It meant she would be off her feet for three months while her body grew new bone. He called it a double plateau tibia fracture. As if that were not enough, she also suffered a spinal compression fracture, causing the muscles to ripple in her back.

With surgeries and long-term recovery in a nursing care center and then at home, Gena faced at least a year and a half of rehabilitation in regaining the use of her leg. Both Gena and Jack had to surrender their dream of touring Europe. Their focus had shifted out of necessity. Now they wanted God's plan to unfold for them.

For Gena, that meant a struggle with blame.

One night a young man named Dan peeked into Gena's room. No one else was around. She hadn't seen Dan in years and was surprised to see him then.

"The Lord sent me, Gena. I have two words for you. I don't know what the Lord means by this, but maybe you do. He said, 'No fault.'"

Gena understood immediately. Dan's words were a gift to her. She'd been in a wrestling match with blame. She vacillated between (1) blaming the young man for his impetuous driving, (2) blaming Jack for not getting a mirror installed on her bike so she could see the impetuous young man behind her, or (3) blaming herself for pushing past her endurance level just before the trip.

But God said there was no blame. What a relief!

"When you lift blame off yourself and other people and have a no-fault attitude, all that's left is to get well. A no-fault attitude puts you in a position to look forward," said Gena.

Today, restored to health, she looks back with gratitude. Jack cared for her in every way and never complained. He laid his heart and life down for her.

"Often when I made requests, he would say, 'As you wish.' I took to calling him Wesley, and he called me Buttercup," Gena laughed as she referenced the movie *The Princess Bride.*

Amid the suffering, there were many blessings. She had no brain damage, nor was she paralyzed. People brought meals and visited when she was shut in. She has been able to resume her normal life.

During that time, the Scriptures fed her spirit. One of the favorites that sustained her came from the book of Philippians:

"Be anxious for nothing, but in everything by prayer and supplication, with thanksgiving, let your requests be made known to God; and the peace of God, which surpasses all understanding, will guard your hearts and minds through Christ Jesus" (Philippians 4:6–7).

Pity

Pity is an odd thing. Who hasn't seen sorrowful eyes turned away when we have entered a room, or walked by? We don't want anyone else to pity us. We hate the sympathetic look that says they are sorry for us but glad it's not them. We go out of our way to avoid such glances.

At the same time, we are perfectly happy to pity ourselves when things don't go our way.

Once, Callie, a three-year-old, found herself on the discipline end of a parent's disapproval. After the punishment had been administered, the little one lamented, "Poor Callie. Poor Callie." Of course, I wanted to hug her, but could not or I would have undone what her parent had tried to teach her. It has occurred to me often since that maybe that's how it is with us and God. We are determined to do a thing, but it would be harmful to us. When the consequences either stop us or slap us in the face, we lament.

We want to appear strong to others, but we crumple instead. We are pitied.

Sarah Young, in *Jesus Calling*, writing as if in the voice of God, admonishes us about falling into the trap of self-pity:

> Be on guard against the pit of self-pity. When you are weary or unwell, this demonic trap is the greatest danger you face. Don't even go near the edge of the pit. Its edges crumble easily, and before you know it, you are on the way down. It's ever so much harder to get out of the pit than to keep a safe distance from it. That is why I tell you to be on guard.
>
> There are several ways to protect yourself from self-pity. When you are occupied with praising and thanking Me, it is impossible to feel sorry for yourself. Also, the closer you live to Me, the more distance there is between you and the pit. Live in the Light of My Presence by *fixing your eyes on Me*. Then you will be able *to run with endurance the race that is set before you*, without stumbling or falling.[1]

Falling into the pit is so easy. A common fable goes like this: A man walked down the street and fell into a pit. He got out and went his way. The next day, he walked down the street and fell into the pit again. Shouldn't he have learned a lesson? The following day, he walked down the street, saw the pit, and walked around it. And the next day, the man walked down a different street. The man finally used his common sense and avoided the pit altogether!

Contrary to the man, we don't need to deal with the pit at all. As *Jesus Calling* states, we can be on guard instead. We can put distance between us and the pit because we know Jesus has already taken care of it. We take our eyes off the circumstances of the pit (that cause our self-pity) and turn them onto Jesus.

He tells us to think about what we understand to be true. We are His. He will never leave our side. He will protect us and love us always. If we are spending our time with Him and believing what we know to be true, then we don't have to carry misery around on our backs. Jesus carries it on His back in our place.

As our events crash in around us in this world, we keep our eyes on Jesus. Only through Him can calmness instead of self-pity reign in our spirits when we endure injustice and suffering. Jesus calls each of us to allow His light to shine through us in any way that will further His kingdom. It may not look very inviting. We may not understand the why of it. We may not see the result. But He calls us to be light in the darkness.

The Old Testament prophet Jeremiah gives us insight about true sorrow as we look to God to supply our need: "The Lord is good to those who wait for Him, to the soul who seeks Him. It is good that one should hope and wait quietly for the salvation of the Lord" (Lamentations 3:25–26).

Stress

A song in the Christian music industry starts out with a staccato beat as the singer belts out that he starts the day running at ninety miles an hour to try to complete his to-do list for the day. After a minute or so, the tempo changes and becomes almost ethereal as the performer hears God's quiet voice in his soul: "Breathe , just breathe . . . just be."[2]

Most of us are barely hanging on while living the staccato life. We try to keep up with what comes before us each day. Keeping the schedule seems to be the mantra.

Some of us are barely hanging on because we've gone through a major life change. We don't know what the "new normal" is supposed to be.

Stress. A way of life.

I can imagine stress feeling a little like the scabs that Job scraped away with the sharp, serrated pieces of pottery. The worries of what is happening in our world, our future, relationship, duties, or making a living can form itchy scabs of pus on our souls. They drive us crazy. How can we scratch them? No matter how hard we scrape, the itch keeps diving deeper and deeper.

When the stress of desolation and hopelessness weighs heavily on our spirits, where is the way up again? Especially when misery upon misery seems to fall upon us, we wonder, *Is there no end?*

What is stress doing to us?

I have a friend who says, "Breathing is an option." I think she means to slow down and quit holding your breath. Life is too fast-paced these days. Like the singer in the above song, I tend to hold my breath as I rush through my days. I don't think I am the only one rushing.

I like the story of Elisha in the Old Testament. His life changed in a whirlwind and was never the same. It shows me how God orchestrates change in our lives in order to point us in a new direction. If our spiritual eyes are locked on God, whether we understand at the time or not, we may find ourselves walking into something incredible.

Elisha spent a lot of time with his mentor, Elijah the prophet, who asked Elisha what he could do for him.

"Please let a double portion of your spirit be upon me," Elisha answered.

"You have asked a hard thing," Elijah declared. "However, if you see me when I am taken from you, it shall be so for you; but if not, it shall not be so."

What courage it must have taken for Elisha to ask such a thing from a great man!

In the story, God took Elijah to heaven in a fiery chariot traveling via whirlwind. Elisha, his apprentice prophet, was walking side by side with him. Elisha would not leave his mentor's side, and he saw it all happen. The Scriptures say it was *sudden*.

I would think Elisha felt his life *suddenly* turned every which way. He was a student prophet, learning how to listen to God and then interpret to the people what God said. He was reaching for the vision of God's call on his life when his teacher was *suddenly* taken away in a wild and crazy moment.

What must Elisha have felt? "I can't do this!" he might have cried. But the next verse says he tore his own clothes into two pieces and grasped the mantle of Elijah that fell as he left earth. Elisha had his eyes on what God was doing all the time.

Then he went to the Jordan River where he began his ministry and became a very great prophet of Israel. He did not lose sight of what God was doing, even after the whirlwind turned his life upside down in a moment. He moved right on through it to the call of God on his life—still reaching for the vision before him.

I bet he was breathing in and out, in and out, the way we are designed to do. He knew that God oversaw his life.

So—does God really forget us? Are His eyes turned somewhere else, making Him unable to see our stress? Of course not. God is always present with us and sees our anxieties. We worry about everything; then our bodies tend to get sick, and our minds and emotions become depressed.

This is no way to live!

Instead, if we consider what God may be doing in our lives instead of worrying about the circumstances we are enduring—what might be ahead for us?

Elisha dug deep for his courage when he asked Elijah to grant him a double portion of the prophet spirit. He had a dream, but it would take courage. He asked anyway.

"Please let a double portion of your spirit be upon me" (2 Kings 2:9).

Courage

Fist shaking often becomes our mode of communication with God—and sometimes with those around us—when difficulties come.

No one will dispute that it takes courage to move forward. Many times we can't choose our circumstances, but we can choose how we will meet them. We work our way through stages of grief and reactions.

During times of intense pressure, God has given His Word, the Scriptures, for us to draw on in order to contend with those forces that would come against us. We may be assaulted by difficulties on the outside, but with Scriptures going through our hearts and minds, we can combat the hatred of the Evil One.

In the end, it comes down to a choice. We can choose to continue in anger, grief, or a myriad of emotions; or we can choose to believe God is working behind the scenes on our behalf. We must remember that God is working everything to our good and we are called according to the purpose He has for us (Romans 8:28).

This must mean our adversities have eternal purpose. Whatever we are dealing with has an impact upon our lives and the lives of others. But we can't see it—like the way Mr. and Mrs. Job could not see the purpose behind their suffering. We benefit today when we read about it. God was proving a man to be faithful, though the devil did all he could to destroy him. Yet Job did not sin.

We can see the purpose, but Job and his wife could not.

At the same time, Mrs. Job crumbled under the load. I like to think God gently led her from her despair to courage. Do we have the courage it takes to trust that God *does* have a plan He is working out for the greater good of ourselves and/or others—even if it takes a great amount of time? After all, this life on earth is a training ground for eternity.

Xochitl Dixon, writing in *Our Daily Bread*, recounted how her friend Kim battled through two consecutive life-threatening diagnoses of cancer. Kim grieved and sobbed her prayers. But the time came when Kim surrendered her situation to God. At that point, she "radiated contagious joy and peace." It didn't mean the situation miraculously cleared up according to her earthly expectations, but Kim's suffering gave her a testimony of hope. "Even when we're in dire circumstances, God can turn our wailing into dancing."[3]

"Weeping may endure for a night, but joy comes in the morning" (Psalm 30:5).

"You have turned for me my mourning into dancing; You have put off my sackcloth and clothed me with gladness" (Psalm 30:11).

Move into courage to seek God no matter what. He's given us the power to make the choices. It's up to us to decide how we will live out our hardships. God has great things in mind for us in eternity.

When we do resolve to let God drive our direction, we may encounter some incredible adventures. We may discover He has plans for us that are grander than the ones we devise for ourselves. If we would possess the courage to trade our ideas for His plans, then we could exchange the drifting in our lives for the purposes He has for us. God promises us over and over in His Word, the Bible, that He will unfold the world to us when we follow His strategies for living instead of our own.

Perhaps your life is spinning out of control, and you can't change the situation. Something is terribly broken, and trusting God seems to be a risky business. Resist the urge to *do something*. Wait for God's deliverance. Pray through the paralysis. When you can't formulate a plan, God can.

When scary events have piled on, I have often wanted to hide. Courage in the face of opposition, no matter what direction it comes from, seems so far away. Hiding seems easier at the time, but it's harder to live with in the long run. Anonymity can become a habit. Facing the threat makes my mouth dry and my heart palpitate, but when we face the challenge, we can hold up our heads and walk in the rescue God brings.

It takes courage to hold on in frightening times. It's a risk. But when we accept that risk, God covers us and sees us through to a wise resolution. Looking back, we wonder why we were afraid.

Waiting takes courage.

Our God promises to be with us—all the time, no matter what. This is our comfort, our confidence, and our courage. We trust Him to infuse us with courage to do something new and untried. Then, we can offer our praise.

Remember—your times are in the hands of God. He alone holds all authority and power. He uses it for your good—to give you a future and a hope, because His love for you is so great. Take courage and lean into Him. His arms are strong and powerful. His body is a bulwark against all adversity, whether it's from within or without. His love is like sunshine, enfolding you in its warmth. Jesus *is* the Son and the Light, the Breath of Life and the Healer. Trust Him. He knows you. This knowing goes right through your soul. He knows you better than you know yourself. He knows where you are right now and why you are the way you are.

"I would have lost heart, unless I had believed that I would see the goodness of the Lord in the land of the living. Wait on the Lord; be of good courage, and He shall strengthen your heart; wait, I say, on the Lord" (Psalm 27:13–14).

Jane's Story

Jane had to find courage somewhere when she faced extremity. In distress, she handed in her notice—effective immediately—to her employer. Praying for God to show up for her in this situation and trying to hold back the tears, Jane explained to her employer the tough situation she lived in. Her employer understood the challenges Jane faced and accepted her resignation, as presented—effective immediately.

The employer then put her arm around Jane and said, "Count me as your friend. I've been in similar circumstances. I can babysit for you so you can have some time to yourself, and I would love for us to do some fun things together sometime."

Jane came out of that interview laughing through her tears with gratitude. Not only did God smooth a path she feared to tread, but He gave her a friend. Jane fully plans to cultivate that new friendship.

"You will show me the path of life; in Your presence is fullness of joy; at Your right hand are pleasures forevermore" (Psalm 16:11).

Provision

We have been trained to think of arranging for provisions when we go someplace. If we are backpacking, then we put our food, bedrolls, and all the paraphernalia we will need on our backs. If we go camping, we pack tents, sleeping bags, chairs, food (in and out of coolers)—and maybe a boat and the trailer to lug it along. Perhaps we go to the ocean; then it's another set of supplies. If we are merely going to work, we pack along another bagful of stuff. We wouldn't want to forget our lunch or a book to read while eating it!

We are trained to provide for ourselves. But how well do we prepare our souls for the journeys of life that we are walking every day? And when the disasters of life come that take away our ability to support ourselves—what then?

God tells us He will provide for us if we ask. He's given us His very Name to call upon. In His Name is every answer we will ever need. I once heard a preacher say that "God's love backs you up." I like that; I like knowing God has my back.

Often, we are completely helpless in our circumstances. We may feel we are in a box with no way out. We fiercely wish we could do something! Circumstances seem to be lined up to trap us.

We must choose a direction for action. If only we could plan for this contingency or that, but most of the time we can't. We don't know which way the dominoes will fall or which way to jump.

Sometimes it's like being the frightened child in the dark, wondering if Daddy will come.

Daddy God comes every time we cry for Him. He brings His comfort in the dark. He brings joy amid pain. He gives us courage to take a step when we feel paralyzed. He soothes our hearts like an earthly Daddy's comforting hug.

Yes, God is with us through everything. He is closer than we can imagine. He never leaves us alone—especially when we feel alone and afraid. There are no other hands so trustworthy as His. In disaster, He holds us close. *Trust His hands.*

How do we put our faith in Him when trouble looms LARGE? We must look beyond the present troubles and anxieties and do what He told us to do. Faith isn't a feeling. Like love, it is a decision we make. God has provided His Word for our instruction, and that means we decide to act on what He says instead of what we see.

Can we sustain belief when everything looks *dark*? We must read God's Word daily and purpose in our hearts to agree with what it says, no matter what difficulty stands in front of us. Is this easy? Heck, no! We are on earth where the truth is often unseen. Truth is still truth, even if the lies are glaringly apparent. The promises of God are still true in every dangerous circumstance and with every dangerous opponent.

Will He come through for us when we DOUBT? This is the crux of the matter. God will always do what is best for us. It may not look like what we wanted or expected, but God always acts with love in response to our utterances directed His way.

He will fight for us!

We can be thankful because our great and wonderful God has made us in His image and constantly gives us His tender care and provision.

Paul wrote, "For though I am absent in the flesh, yet I am with you in spirit, rejoicing to see your good order and the steadfastness of your faith in Christ. As you therefore have received Christ Jesus the Lord, so walk in Him, rooted and built up in Him and established in the faith, as you have been taught, abounding in it with thanksgiving" (Colossians 2:5–7).

What does His provision for us look like?

Steadfast Faith: God declares He is *for* us. He rejoices over our steadfast faith when we believe He is *for* us. He invites us to walk closely with Him in companionship.

Rooted in Truth: When we believe He is with us and He is *for* us, we become rooted in truth. We gain assurance, and we can be confident.

Built Up: We can become open to great things He wants to build up in us. He gives us dreams to follow and gifts to work with in accomplishing those dreams.

Established: He establishes us in our faith and leads us in the direction He wants our lives to take. He has redeemed our very lives and fashions us to live free and with honor.

Abounding: Finally, like Jabez in the Old Testament (1 Chronicles 4:10), God gives us the ability to abound. He enlarges our boundaries, and we can follow His great adventure anywhere He takes us.

God is *for* us!

Diane's Story

Diane needed her job. It seemed that she always teetered on the edge of layoffs.

Living on her own, she supported chickens, dogs, cats, and other critters on her rural property. She loved her animals and felt that God called her to provide sanctuary for them, as well as for the wilder creatures that foraged for food around her.

But Diane's unstable employment kept her feeling like a yo-yo. She also felt keenly the separation that losing her job would cause. Though she loved living in the country with her furry and feathered friends, it did cause some isolation. Not going to work daily and sharing interaction with her human friends could wrap her life in loneliness.

Years before, Diane had worked for a company for several years before a layoff derailed her. She'd loved that job; it was more than just employment. She'd had opportunities to interact with people around the world and learn of their interesting lives. After sharing many affectionate friendships at this workplace, being cut off had wounded her. She did find another job, allowing her to use her talents in diverse ways, but the family feeling simply wasn't there.

Diane's worst fears materialized, and she was once again without means to support herself. She looked for work. She had a mortgage, a car payment, and all the usual bills—but no income. And in all of this, she worried about her critters. How would she provide for them?

She cried out to God—what would He do for her?

Surely He loved her animals more than she did.

While waiting for God to deliver a means of support, Diane filled in anywhere she could in order to make some money to pay her bills, all the while praying for His provision.

Diane struggled for nearly a year and a half, but then a placement opened up at her favorite place of employment, and she was asked if she would consider returning. *Would* she? Yes, of course! Once more, she could do the job she'd always loved. Her work had meaning. Her life had value. She could feel God's love in this provision. Her friends welcomed her back with joy.

While Diane's financial struggles did not completely disappear, she was grateful to God. He had been faithful to restore her to the employment she loved and the friends who were like family to her.

And her critters were safe.

Friendships and Intercession

More than once, friends have changed my outlook—and therefore my life—during dark times. Their hugs have warmed me, and their words have encouraged me to keep going.

Being alone only reinforced the gloom when I pushed away those who would come around me. It's important for us to continue friendships during tough phases in our lives. An image often referring to difficult times is the crushing of grapes in order to release the sweet juice within them. As we take our turn in the winepress, sweet friendships matter very much. There are no substitutes for hugs. Let them come!

When bad things happen to friends and loved ones, don't back off. Press in, even if it means just sitting side by side in silence for a time. It's hard to stand in the gap for someone we love. They are in the harsh place, and we want to assist but don't see how. Will we harm or help with our good intentions? No matter our fears, when we press in, relationships are strengthened.

Instead of offering judgment, we can call on our empathy and pray for them. We look from the outside in, but only God comprehends what they may be enduring.

We have been given the tools we need. He has given us His own Spirit to discern distress in the lives of those around us. He's given us love to care for them, a sound mind to think for them when or if they cannot think straight, and power to stand by their side, no matter what spirit of fear may try to interfere.

"God has not given us a spirit of fear, but of power and of love and of a sound mind" (2 Timothy 1:7).

Oswald Chambers, in *My Utmost for His Highest*, said, "Worship and intercession must go together, the one is impossible without the other. Intercession means that we rouse ourselves up to get the mind of Christ about the one for whom we pray."[4]

Intercession often clears our minds of our own troubles as we focus on others.

If Mrs. Job's life had lacked spiritual depth, her husband's rebuke could have jolted her with a wake-up call. She became aware of a need for prayer, both for herself and her husband.

Often our hearts change as we follow a daily practice of prayer. God may give us inspiration about our own condition or that of someone else. Mrs. Job could have been surprised at the compassion she came to feel for her husband, even though her own situation was nearly as dire as his.

When we lack the emotions, we can allow God to move in and love others through us.

Through intercession, we can determine in our sound mind that we will love others, do for them, and care for them—and suddenly, one day we will find it's not forced, but real.

Fran's Story

Fran was a single mom. Anyone who has gone through trauma that leaves you alone to raise your children can understand how devastating this can be. Fran's little girl was about four years old. Fran wondered how she would be able to do this parenting thing by herself. Children need so much. Fran worried about working her day job in order to provide basic needs. Could she still come home with energy and patience to be present for a bouncing, active child?

She felt inadequate for the job. Exhaustion would set in, obstacles loomed, and Fran was alone. As a new Christian, she had heard how God answers prayer. Would He do that for her if she prayed a purely practical prayer for help?

She met a new acquaintance. A single lady had recently moved into Fran's neighborhood and was missing a close chum she'd left behind when she'd moved. This lady had prayed for a new friend. That person became Fran. Both women were able to come alongside each other to help with practical things women living on their own must handle. Encouragement, girl-talk, and fun came in the deal as well. Fran did not need to worry about her child, either, because her friend supported and helped her with her child as well as offering friendship.

God did not disappoint Fran. He brought her a companion to share trials and good times with, as well as mentoring in her Christian walk.

Meditation Questions

1. At a time when life seemed to fall apart and you didn't understand, did you experience some fist shaking?
2. When you feel abandoned by God, how do you deal with it?
3. When have you pitied yourself? What did you do with it?
4. What does it take for you to call upon God in a stressful time?
5. Do you see your adverse circumstances as testings to grow your dependence on God?
6. Can you remember a time when you prayed for someone when you didn't feel like it, only to find that, over time, your feelings changed?

Journal Question

A suggestion for defusing stress:

Take some time to sit in your yard and feel the soft breeze touch you as it floats by. Feel the warmth of the sun on your toes. Listen to the birdsong, and watch the clouds drift. God is with you in the secret garden of your heart.

Write down what you observe and feel. End your journal time by writing praises to God.

At a future stress time, you might read again what you wrote this day.

God is faithful.

Prayer

"And he took for himself a potsherd with which to scrape himself while he sat in the midst of the ashes" (Job 2:8).

Lord, thank You that You never leave us, no matter what happens. Only Your presence can bring true comfort in our dark times. Give us the courage to live as You would have us live. Thank You for the provisions You make for our good. Help us to "pay it forward" as we come alongside those who suffer and need a warm hug. You are faithful, kind, good, generous, and loving. Praise You, Lord Jesus.

THREE

Repentance and Forgiveness

Shall we indeed accept good from God,
and shall we not accept adversity?
Job 2:10

It could have happened this way . . .

Even as her arm lowered, Mrs. Job seethed. She watched her fingers flex, and she heard the pottery scrapes in the silence. She wanted to scream in frustration! Bending over, Mrs. Job picked up the broom and quietly replaced it in the corner. She had to get away for a while!

She pulled her shawl from the peg next to the broom and stared. A peg. On the wall. In a single-room dwelling. A simple, patched shawl—patched by her own hand, no less. She stifled a snort, tossed the covering over her head, and scooted around her husband, who was still sitting in the doorway. Neither of them said a word.

Mrs. Job strode out into the dirt street and began her trek, weaving around the openings denoting places of residence much like her own. Beggars, merchants leading animals with loads on their backs, and stalls with fly-infested food lined the other side. To protect herself from the dusty air, she covered her nose and mouth with her shawl. Otherwise, Mrs. Job paid no attention to the activity around her. Stormy-faced, she kept her thoughts locked inside.

God, where are You?

Pulling her shawl closer around her face, she hurried on by the city gates. She did not want anyone recognizing her. Job used to sit on the terraces above the gates where his former associate judges now sat. Perhaps they were busy with the humanity crowding around them and would not notice a lone woman like her. *The hypocrites!*

She passed the stairs leading to the upper levels of the city, but barely glanced at them. Up there was no place for her anymore. She hustled by.

Finally, she came to a dried-up garden, saw no one there, and sat on the mud-brick bench to let the tears fall. No one tended this garden or watered the plants. She felt at home. At least no one would notice her, and for that she was grateful.

Doesn't he understand? she moaned.

Of course he does.

His look had been kind, but his words firm: "You speak as one of the foolish women."

Mrs. Job adjusted her veil to give her face more shade. He had said she *spoke* like a foolish woman—not that she *was* a foolish woman. She sat up straighter.

"Shall we indeed accept good from God, and shall we not accept adversity?" Her husband's words seeped into her heart. She wiped her eyes and nose with a corner of her wrap.

She was guilty.

She *did* expect only good from God. Her life had been blessed. She'd grown up in a well-to-do family and married well. Job was recognized far and wide for his wisdom, his honest business practices, and his kindness to those who served him. When he had proposed marriage, the bride-price he offered had satisfied her father. She also brought a large dowry to the marriage, as well as some education. Her embroidery brought in an income. She'd been renowned for her embroidery. Now she couldn't afford materials. Mending was not the same thing at all!

Her husband had taught her about his God. Then she and her husband had built a family of ten children. She once held an honored place in society as her husband held an honored place at the city gates.

But that life is over, and only God knows where our lives are going now.

She shifted on the bench and leaned forward with her hands planted on either side of her to support her body. Unmoving, she stared at the mud-brick wall in front of her. She breathed deeply, trying to ease the tension between her shoulders. Out of the corner of one eye, she could see the droopy tree that tried to cover the untended flowerbed. Brown, everywhere she looked. Heat waves passed before her eyes.

Silence reigned in the garden, even as muted voices haggling over goods and animals objecting to treatment drifted over the top of the city walls. Her skin prickled. The shame of her outburst washed over her. Job had not deserved that. He had always been kind to her. How could she have let her thoughts erupt against him like that?

He had never—no, not once—let an angry word escape his lips. He had been gentle and compassionate toward her in their grief, selflessly helping her through the transition from living high in the city to groveling at the bottom. He continued to worship his God.

Mrs. Job sighed and bowed her head to whisper. "Oh, Most High. I am trying to accept that You are sovereign. I did not understand. I still don't understand. Job remains faithful to You. What did he mean when he said we must accept adversity as well as good from Your hand?"

Pressure rose in her chest and tears welled in her eyes. "If he can keep worshiping You even now, then help me to grasp that You are sovereign, as my husband believes."

The pressure forced the tears to flow, and she covered her face as her shoulders shook. She wept quietly.

"Help me to understand that You have a right to do whatever You wish. Please help me."

She gulped back a final sob, stood, and set her face for home.

Meanwhile, in the book of Job . . .

As we saw in Scripture, Satan strutted into the throne room, and God commented on Job's faithfulness. With a win over God in mind, the adversary's response was predictable. When God granted Satan permission to strike Job's person but not to kill him, Satan must have left the presence of God gleefully, already counting on his win.

The key to remember is that the devil cannot do anything without God's permission. If we did not know that before, this very verse assures us of it. God is always in control. The devil must ask permission. So why does God allow bad things? Aside from the fact that we live in a fallen world, we may never discern the answers on this side of heaven. Can we be okay with this? Can we trust that God knows what He is doing with us—His own creation?

When Job broke out in painful boils all over his body, sitting in ashes and scratching the itching skin, he must have been extremely uncomfortable.

He had declared that good things as well as adversity come

from God. The Scriptures say that in all of this, Job did not sin with his lips. His trust and devotion in his God were so complete that Job laid down his life and his expectations before Him.

Facing Rebuke

Perhaps after Mrs. Job's famous outburst, when Job looked at her and responded in defense of God, her heart was cut to the quick. Did she—like Peter after he denied Jesus—go off by herself and weep bitterly?

Where Job's story spoke of faithfulness, Mrs. Job's story could be one of struggle. Her life of privilege disappeared in a moment, and her bitter heart expressed itself when she blamed God. Who of us couldn't relate?

Her husband's words caught her short. What could she say then? I think she had no other recourse but to rush from the house to examine what had just happened. Perhaps she wept over how low her emotions had sunk.

What might Mrs. Job have learned from her husband's rebuke? Possibly she heard the voice of God in it. How could she accept adversity as well as good from the hand of God?

Can God trust us with a rebuke?

Words of truth had pierced Mrs. Job's heart, exposing her anger, sadness, and disappointment in God. As a result, she could have speculated what she should do about it. Perhaps she struggled with the blame she had assigned to God as she questioned how He could have taken all ten of her children away from her at once.

Job accused his wife of speaking like a foolish woman. We all strive with our tongues. I can't count the number of times I wanted to snatch back words I had spoken. If I didn't hear the rebuke instantly in my mind, someone would surely point it out later. I don't always take it very well. After all, who are they to judge me?

I hate to think of myself as a foolish woman, but there is nothing that makes us look or feel more foolish than wayward words from our own mouths.

It could be that God uses rebukes for our good so that we might repent, apologize, or make it right in some other way.

What is harder than facing ourselves? Do we ever really get a true picture? We blame others for causing us to do something instead of putting blame where it belongs. Or we consider ourselves the scum of the earth for our misdeeds or thoughts.

It took the rebuke of her husband to make Mrs. Job look at herself. Once she rejected the foolish-woman identity, she pushed through to honestly assess herself. Yes, she *had* expected only good from God.

Why would He send her anything else? She was a good person. She did all the right things. She'd raised ten prosperous children. She probably ran her household economically in order to support her husband well. She might even have given to the poor.

But it wasn't enough. She had to face her own heart and her attitude toward God. Had she loved and served God, or had she only loved her privileged position in society? It seemed God had another plan for her life, and she had rejected it.

Sometimes it takes retreating, as Mrs. Job did in the barren garden, to understand what God is aiming at in our lives. He may have great insights for us, or He may want us to come to acceptance and trust Him.

These feel like times of darkness in our souls. This is not when despair reigns, but instead it's a gentle time of quietness to sit still and listen. Possibly, then, our spiritual ear is active and hears, or maybe God moves us into a time of darkness when His hand shields us from the world. We sit in our living room with low lights and wait for His insights. Or we sit outside on our porch to watch His creation around us while we wait for His voice. Maybe it's not words that come. Perhaps it's just a gentle warmth. We are assured He is with us.

Oswald Chambers says, "Then remain quiet. If you open your mouth in the dark, you will talk in the wrong mood; darkness is a time to listen."[1]

It is a sacred time when the soul waits upon the Spirit.

Chambers makes this point: "God does not tell you what He is going to do; He reveals to you who He is."[2]

After being rebuked, Mrs. Job fled to a lonely place in solitude to examine herself. Her soul was troubled and angry. Out of her confused state, she'd lashed out at her husband. She may have cried out to God from the depths of her anguished being, but she came back quiet and restored.

God always sees us and hears us—every day, all the time. He sees our coming in and our going out. He is intimately involved in our thought processes and in the details of our day-to-day living. He sees us. He may not tell us His plans for us, but He promises never to leave or forsake us—in the light or in the dark.

It may take some time, but it's safe to repent of our deeds. We humbly place ourselves before God with no excuses, acknowledging His sovereignty.

Most likely, it's not punishment we receive, but His mercy and love.

"But may the God of all grace, who called us to His eternal glory by Christ Jesus, after you have suffered a while, perfect, establish, strengthen, and settle you" (1 Peter 5:10).

Janet's Story

On a mild day in Los Angeles, Janet and her friend Linda took a walk. Linda's two-year-old child had cerebral palsy, and Janet offered to push his stroller. As part of their faith, they often passed out gospel tracts as they walked.

This day during their stroll, they noticed a man by the railroad tracks. He was rough looking and noticeably agitated and fidgety.

His manner intimidated the two women, and Janet was particularly concerned for the baby.

"What's up with him?" they whispered to each other. "He's pretty scary looking."

They stepped up their pace.

Suddenly, Janet felt a distinct impression that God wanted her to stop and witness to this lost-looking guy.

Disturbed, she argued inwardly: "No, Lord. I have to protect the baby." She and Linda quickened their strides away from the man. Glancing over her shoulder at him, she saw him muttering to himself and making jerking movements. Unease began to shadow Janet.

Later in the evening, Janet saw a news clip on the television. Her heart was pierced as she heard about a man who had jumped in front of a moving train to end his life. She covered her face with her hands as guilt washed over her. It was possible the dead man was not the man she had seen earlier that day, but Janet *knew* it was him. She could almost hear the Lord's voice saying, "I told you to witness to him."

The rebuke washed through her. She'd had a chance to make a difference to that stranger, but she had walked away.

"The conviction was so strong," she says, "that I felt like I was a partaker in his suicide. I could have given him hope."

Over time, Janet has come to a place of receiving forgiveness. She knows God has forgiven her, and she has forgiven herself. The severe guilt has gone, but the memory lingers.

"I should have listened, but I didn't. It was a learning experience. Never think you have arrived or know everything, because God is still teaching.

"When we have a knowledge of the Scriptures, we know that the Lord wants us to always be ready to preach the gospel to the lost, yet fear kept me from doing what I knew to do. I should have trusted that God would keep us safe. There was no real danger."

The lasting lesson for Janet has been, "Don't second-guess the Spirit of God. He knows what He is talking about if He asks you to do something. Just trust Him and do it."

Janet learned the truth of this Scripture: "Trust in the Lord with all your heart, and lean not on your own understanding" (Proverbs 3:5).

Like Mrs. Job, Janet came away from her experience of rebuke quiet and restored. God is always waiting for us to learn from Him.

Managing Expectations

Certainly, we would always choose good things for ourselves and our loved ones. Good things enhance our lives. We want our loved ones to be happy. How could it be otherwise? God is good. The Scriptures tell us in Genesis that God declared all He made good.

But when adversity comes, how are we to react? We get stuck. Adversity appears to be the opposite of the good.

Illness strikes and a child's life hangs in the balance. The loss of a job means the death of a dream—a career seems to spiral downward. Loved ones die. Natural disasters rob us of everything.

Disappointment in God comes easily to us when our lives go south. What is He doing? How do we get from disappointment to the kind of trust Job had in God—a trust that recognizes God is sovereign and can do as He wills?

In the midst of trouble, Job asks, "Shall we indeed accept good from God, and shall we not accept adversity?"

The truth is that none of us are in command. Only God really knows what tapestry He is weaving among His creation. Like Mrs. Job, we can come to the place of acceptance and manage how we will go forward from this point, or we can continue to fight the inevitable that comes upon us. The struggle is real, but surrender can bring new growth.

It looks dark, but it's in that dark condition where germination takes place. New life will put out its feelers in the manure-treated dirt. The scrawny kernel pushes upward until the sun touches it, the rain seeps in, and it grows.

My family grew a garden in a good-sized backyard lot. One year we ordered a pile of manure to fertilize the ground before growing the luscious vegetables that we harvested in the autumn. We had dreams of cornstalks taller than us and constantly producing green beans.

When the manure pile was delivered, my six-year-old daughter scrunched up her face in distaste.

"What is *that*, Mom?"

"That's manure."

"What's manure?"

"Cow poop."

She looked at the pile, and then at me in amazement. "Oh, come on, Mom. What is it *really*?"

"It's cow poop," I repeated.

She paused, still considering the pile. "Are you telling the truth?"

Holding in my laughter, I worked hard to convince her that it really was cow poop. I think the only reason she finally believed me was because of the smell.

There is no mistaking the stink of cow poop!

Often, we harbor self-centered expectations that resemble manure. By itself, it reeks! But when it is turned into the ground, it nourishes new plants—plants that God raises from the dead. When we surrender our selfish expectations, what an abundance of sweet produce is yielded!

Just as the manure comes before the garden, so it is in our souls. As we examine earthly expectations in our souls, we have the choice of spreading dung or allowing the Master Gardener to till the soil of our souls until the manure is absorbed. Then He plants us like bulbs and seeds that will spring up and cause us to be a sweet-smelling aroma to whomever we come into contact with.

Jesus came to die for our sins. His body went into the tomb. Then, like the bulb waiting in the dark for the sun before it bursts forth in beautiful colors, Jesus rose from the tomb to give us life everlasting. He shares His continual love and life instructions for us in the Bible.

Talk to God constantly. Keep Him in the loop of your life. Examine your soul daily. What are the thoughts floating around in your head? Name them, put them where they need to go, and release them. I find journaling helps to get those thoughts out where I can see them. Surrender your expectations, and choose to move forward in His plan.

It's always better than the plans we choose for ourselves.

Marie's Story

Marie's marriage provided her life's training ground. She'd had a dream of what a happy marriage should look like: an attentive husband, her role as a good wife and mother—all with great contentment. But reality did not match up. Once married, Jake, her husband, neither saw nor heard her.

"I didn't want to believe he didn't really care, and I was sure I could handle it," Marie insisted. "Pride would not let me admit otherwise."

As Jake became increasingly wrapped up in his own life, Marie noticed other unusual behaviors and mental issues, not only toward her, but toward his original family. Over time, through his neglect and hurtful words, she lost her sense of identity and became an appendage to make Jake's life work.

"I tried to get help. But as far as Jake was concerned, he would never acknowledge that there were any problems. I dealt with it by shutting down emotionally." Like the fruit from which the juice has been squeezed, Marie had been emptied of her life.

"Denial is powerful," Marie continued with her story. "I handled things by trying to be everything to everyone in my family." By this time, two sons had been added to their household. The boys grew older, and Marie found herself trying to referee conflicts between Jake and their boys as his behaviors escalated. She tried to formulate plans of escape for herself and the boys should it become a paramount need.

Marie became angry and afraid. With tensions at home and feeling isolated by a lack of friends or anyone to come alongside her, she pulled into herself and did not tell anyone of her private anguish. The manure was piling up, and Marie could hardly stand the stink.

Finally, driven by desperation and panic attacks, Marie did two things: she cried out to God and committed to work with a counselor. God forgave her own sins and her attempts to manage the unmanageable in her own strength. The counselor gave her tools to move forward and crawl out of the manure.

"I thank God for forgiveness and for showing me myself in so many gentle and noncondemning ways so I could start weeding out the negatives in my life," Marie said about the changes she needed to make in herself.

Marie developed a longing for truth. She started talking to people she trusted. She learned that her honesty proved her motives to herself, and she could move forward. As she realized she had friends praying for her, some of her burdens were lifted from her soul.

Through studies, she gained insight and began to live in the truths she discovered. Freedom was visible!

The Bible came alive for Marie. She found out that the words of the Scriptures are also tools for spiritual warfare. As she learned to pray through everything, God amazed her with peace during her storms. She began to believe that God really did love her and that she had worth because of His love—even if her husband did not love or appreciate her.

She held Scripture in her mind. In particular, this verse calmed her over and over: "I hold on to you for dear life, and you hold me steady as a post" (Psalm 63:8 MSG).

"It was a whole new way of living." Marie's excitement bubbled forth. "God is my strength through turbulent times and always."

Her circumstances did not change overnight. Her heart continued to be bashed, but the way opened for Marie to run to the one who could keep her from hardening her heart again.

Eventually, the marriage ended. Marie had help through counseling and support from her church. During this process, one night as Marie drifted off to sleep, she sensed another danger. "There was the ugliest face, black and floating above me, telling me how worthless I really am. I was afraid and yelled, 'Jesus, help!' Just that soon, the ugly presence was gone. I slept peacefully. Once again, it was Jesus to my rescue."

Marie needed a hero. She read in the book of Revelation that Jesus rides a white horse. She clung to the verse and to the Hero whom she had discovered: "Now I saw heaven opened, and behold, a white horse. And He who sat on him was called Faithful and True, and in righteousness He judges and makes war" (Revelation 19:11).

Give and Take

Anger is such a difficult emotion to master. It may boil over in fury and cause destruction around us, as it did for Mrs. Job. Or it may take a more controlled channel, calm and deadly.

On the other hand, anger could be the conduit to recognizing wrong and addressing it for a healing purpose.

Discerning the differences between righteous anger and sinful anger is no easy task. David Jeremiah explains it well in his blog post "Understanding the Difference between Righteous and Sinful Anger."[3]

He says, "We can't prevent situations in life where we are tempted to exhibit 'life rage,' but that doesn't mean we have to yield to the temptation."[4]

He urges us to monitor our anger. Is your temper ready to boil? What is the cause? How can you diffuse it? Be careful of your words.

Does your anger simmer beneath the surface? Search your soul for thoughts of revenge or other dangerous, wrathful ideas that might lurk there.

Do you feel as if God has wronged you? Does this get in the way of your worship of Him?

Dr. Jeremiah says the key to managing anger is to daily ask the Holy Spirit to fill us with His power to control our feelings, as described in His Word. Listing the fruit of the Spirit, Paul concludes with "gentleness, self-control," adding, "against such there is no law" (Galatians 5:23).

On the other hand, righteous anger often carries with it the desire to right a wrong. In this case, Dr. Jeremiah says, "You are responding to the violation of a righteous standard of God. You are reacting to the influence of sin in our world. You are angry that Satan and his agents have such devastating influence. You are feeling righteous indignation."[5]

When Jesus traveled to Jerusalem and walked into the temple, He expressed His righteous indignation by turning over the money tables. He declared, "It is written, 'My house is a house of prayer,' but you have made it a 'den of thieves'" (Luke 19:46).

God's house had become a marketplace. The real reason for the temple was lost in commerce. When Jesus saw it, His anger burned hot until He expressed it in a way that would bring change—or at least recognition of the wrong of compromising the worship of God.

After examining her own anger against God, Mrs. Job could have endured some character deepening. Can we say no to character deepening? And if so, at what cost?

Once we face our anger, where do we direct it? Trusting God to deal rightly with those injustices that make us angry doesn't come overnight. Often, we pray and think we have "given it to God," but we are really seeking other alternatives to correct what is wrong. We think we can control the situation, but it only leads to more worry, more anger, and more bondage.

Is it over for us when we blow it? Because we will. No! He carefully and gently guides us through to the other side of our dark experience. His mercy is showcased in our lives, just as it was in the lives of Job and his wife.

Examine your heart and pour out all the resentment before God. He can take it. He knows how to work it through to a righteous conclusion and restore you to Himself and others. Even if your circumstances don't change, your heart can change when it's in His hands.

Brenda's Story

Brenda's ordered life began to change when she received a call from a teacher alerting her to daughter Breanna's seventh-grade social life.

"Be careful. Breanna is getting into a tough crowd."

Brenda was shaken. "It was the first inkling I had that Bre was experiencing things I knew nothing about." Brenda and Bryan had three girls, Breanna (the eldest), Lindsee, and Whitney.

"As parents, we tend to think we have control of our children. We hope they will grow up with a good, moral character. Bryan and I posted a list of traits in our kitchen for our children to strive for in order to have a successful life. We called them 'suggestions.' When they wanted to go somewhere or do something, we would ask if it honored God, if the parents of their friends knew their plans, and if it lined up with the 'suggestions.' If the answers were no, they could not do it."

Their list included such suggestions as these:

- Love God.
- Honor our family.
- Be hardworking.
- Don't lie.
- Don't cheat.
- Be trustworthy to all.
- Don't talk about others (gossip).
- Find joy in life.
- Always try your best.
- Know that your best is always enough.

"I always admired Breanna's strong will. I thought it would stand her in good stead as she grew up and would make her a dependable adult. I saw a lot of good qualities, but her strong will was a detriment to her as a thirteen-year-old. She wanted to be in charge of her life—too soon."

When Breanna turned thirteen, the suggestions stayed home, and she went out the door in search of "freedom." Freedom turned out to be a fourteen-year-old boyfriend who came from a rough home with no rules. His time was his own, and he used illegal drugs and drank. Breanna was intrigued; Brenda was aghast. Brenda invited Breanna to bring her friend home since she believed in keeping her enemies close. She tried to get to know the boy.

But Breanna bucked the system at home and ran away.

The first time Breanna left home, Brenda experienced disbelief and fear. How could Bre run away? She had loving parents! How could this happen? Would she be in danger? Where could they look for her?

The second time Breanna left, Brenda was astounded. All she could think was, *Are you KIDDING me?*

By the third time, Brenda and Bryan knew they had to do something. They went to an attorney for advice. He informed them about a CHINS petition. It means "a child in need of services." It's used by the juvenile court to help a child to recognize the consequences of her actions and regulate her behavior. The child would be steered toward a court appearance where a judge could help with enforcing rules. It would also hold parents accountable.

While this did help a little, it did not stop Breanna from running away from home eighteen times before adulthood. Each time, Brenda prayed constantly for Breanna's safety and for her own anger that continued to mount. Underneath, the why question simmered toward God.

Breanna would manipulate people and tell lies about her home-life that haunted Brenda and Bryan. "None of those parents called us to check on the truth of what she told them. I still wonder why," Brenda said as she shook her head.

"We had done all we could to direct and teach her, but we failed. I prayed and prayed. I gave Bre to God over and over. And that's the thing—over and over! I kept taking her back. After all, she was my daughter, and as her parent, I was responsible for her."

Then came the day when the police called. Bryan was out of town on a job, and Brenda was tending to the needs of her younger daughters. Dinnertime was upon them.

"They asked for Breanna's dental records. I was devastated. Bre had been gone for six months this time. Had we lost her?"

Numb, Brenda called the dental office to set the process in motion. Then she turned her attention to Lindsee and Whitney. They must be fed, homework tended to, and bedtime managed. Once they were settled, Brenda went to her own room and fell to her knees.

"I'm a good parent! Why are You doing this to me?"

Between prayers and sobs, Brenda came to see her operating belief—that if you did what you were supposed to do, then God would reward you—was not working. Now what?

When are you going to trust Me? God's voice pierced through Brenda's anguish.

What?

In an instant, she knew this was not about her. "Oh my gosh! Bre was never mine! She always had belonged to God. It was such a wash of relief to me."

The thought kept repeating in her head, "She really wasn't mine. God is in control. I am not. Whatever the police found, Bre is God's. For the first time, I really honestly and completely surrendered Breanna to God. Come what may."

Brenda slept through the night.

The next morning, a friend called to say she saw Breanna walking down the road that morning. She wanted Brenda to know.

Great relief! "God gave me what I needed that morning. I had to know my daughter was still alive."

The girl found at the bottom of a ravine the previous day had been a friend of Breanna's. "It could have been Bre, but God was not done with her."

Two days later, Breanna came home for a while.

"Mom, were you praying for me a couple days ago?"

"Yes."

"Specifically, did you pray for a hedge of protection to surround me?"

"Yes. Why?"

"I was sleeping in a phone booth, and when I woke up, I saw angels all around me."

Breanna was not yet done running, but Brenda's life had changed. She knew now that God had a design for her daughter. It was not Brenda's job to direct and lead her daughter, who in fact belonged to God. Brenda's job had been to love Breanna. She had done all she was given to do as a parent. She could cut the apron strings for good—and not take them back again.

Brenda also understood that Jesus was gently drawing her into a greater relationship with Him.

"If you don't learn, then the Holy Spirit will bring the lesson right back around again. It's sort of like a knot tied at the bottom of a rope, and you are hanging on at the end. God brought Bre's continual running to me as a process to finally surrender everything to Him. I never really understood surrender. I thought I knew what it meant, but I didn't—until the night I thought I'd lost her."

"Fearing and trusting God, no matter what, is most important. Children, our most precious loved ones, come after that."

What Breanna remembers from that time is how her parents always loved her. She has fulfilled the prayer Brenda offered up for her long ago. She is a strong, beautiful, independent, successful woman who knows firmly that God is in control of her life. She now prays for her own children.

"God has blessed us," Brenda says.

When friends who have rebellious teens come to her with their questions, Brenda's response is, "Get on your knees. Totally surrender your children to God, and don't take them back. Trust Him."

"You who fear the Lord, trust in the Lord; He is their help and their shield" (Psalm 115:11).

Forgiveness

After dealing with anger, could it be harder to forgive yourself? I think Mrs. Job thought so. Maybe she feared God would strike her dead. Perhaps she shocked herself by screaming that ugly comment to her husband, but she couldn't curb the angry words. How else could she express her anguish and hopelessness?

Forgiveness is what we must do if we want to move on with our lives and grow in our souls. If we don't forgive, it stunts our growth and gets in the way of worshiping God. However, our emotions and memory often don't cooperate.

But in asking the Holy Spirit for the power to make decisions to live differently, we can choose to forgive. We may not forget, but we are no longer compelled to run the video in our minds. We can squelch it. We can say, "No, I am done with that." We can move on to more productive things and leave the forgetting to God.

Marilyn Meberg, in her book *I'd Rather Be Laughing*, has some suggestions. She says, "We need to mentally separate the act of forgiveness and the act of reuniting. They are not the same. We can forgive our offender and still plan not to see that person again." She suggests, however, that if the offender asks for the forgiveness, a new relationship could be possible.[6] When I mess up, I often hear, "Don't be so hard on yourself." It's probably true that the sin I am beating myself up over is not such a big issue for the other people involved, but to me it is horrendous.

I left a job some years ago. When I handed in my notice to my employer, I was not kind in how I did it; he did not deserve the huff-and-puff show to which I treated him. I cleaned out my desk and left. For years after that, shame festered in my soul. I knew I was held back in some areas of my life because I needed to go back and ask his forgiveness. But year after year, I struggled with my pride. How could I go back? Yes, it had been time for me to leave, but to do it the way I did was wrong.

Finally, the day came when I called and invited my former employer and his wife to my new home. They came. I asked them to forgive me. They graciously did. It was humbling for me, but was such a relief to have it over. The relationship was restored. They extended grace to me. I have been free to move forward. I have praised God for it.

In his book about grace, Max Lucado says, "Grace is not blind.

It sees the hurt full well. But grace chooses to see God's forgiveness even more. It refuses to let hurts poison the heart."[7]

My former employer and his wife are my friends once again. But that day, years ago, they had to deal with my actions and smooth it over with other employees. They had to grieve a broken friendship, but they set that aside to extend the grace of forgiveness to me.

God's voice is sweet, kind, loving, generous, and full of truth. He may give us instructions. We may have to go to those we've wronged and make it right. There is no other way. May we be quick to do so. We may be surprised at the relief and kindness we find on the other side.

Coming to Terms

When things go well, we are happy to serve God. But when things go haywire, we are inclined to do what Mrs. Job did. We cry out against God.

Is He finished with us at this point? NO! He carefully and gently guides us through and out the other side. His mercy is showcased in our lives, as it was in the lives of Job and his wife.

Life is so real, isn't it? Sometimes we feel as if we are on top of the pinnacle, and then, WHAP! We're lying on our back looking up at the sky. Despite our best efforts, we find we are replaying an ugly tape in our minds.

"I should have said . . ."

"If he/she says one more thing . . ."

We could be imagining a total fantasy grievance, building a whole story and reacting to a mental rehearsal of what we want to say. It doesn't matter what it is; we're fighting it. But God doesn't let us go too far, does He? He brings intervention. Something we read. Something we hear. Something we see. Someone who has a word of wisdom for us.

Suddenly, we see where we were headed. The not good place. It's time for a U-turn. Then what happens?

Immense relief!

Cool, soothing waters.

Freedom from cowering fear.

Freedom from oppression.

Covered by God's hand—safe.

Peace amid chaos!

Perhaps the dark place is necessary for our growth. Maybe it must come prior to the next new adventure Father God takes us on. It's dwelling inside the palm of His hand, being protected and readied for the next thing.

Sue's Story

Sue, like Mr. and Mrs. Job, is familiar with the struggle of coming to terms with life when everything is stripped away.

"I'm pretty tough," Sue says. She learned this by surviving childhood abuse. Then she married, had a family, and became a widow—suddenly. Picking up the pieces as she grieved, Sue struggled to provide for her family. During her widowhood, another child was born to her—unplanned.

"This child brought me joy beyond anything," says Sue, yet, facing a pregnancy as a single mom while working in an Ivy League university caused plenty of tension. Sue endured the stigma and disapproval of professional colleagues.

Sue's second marriage twelve years later was a short-lived disaster, destroyed by her husband's alcoholism. Determined to rebuild her life and provide a father for her children, she remarried a third time. However, her third husband found someone else and ended the marriage. She lost her home, and the new girlfriend moved in.

Sue and her husband had been fostering her grandchildren for several years, but the welfare system took them away and forbade her contact with them.

Her mother died within a month after Sue discovered her husband's unfaithfulness. This stirred up old unanswered questions and best-forgotten pain from Sue's relationship with her mother.

Her family gone, her finances destroyed, and her heart broken, Sue immersed herself in her work, directing a large tutoring center at a community college. But only a few years later, disaster struck again when statewide budget cuts mandated the closing of her entire department. Of the last day in her tutoring center, she says, "I looked at the packed boxes of records—ten years of lives that had passed through my domain. Emptiness filled my heart, and I could only sob my anguish. What had defined my life was gone. I was too old for a new start and too young to retire."

Sue was left with nothing. "How does one define loss? Where is the bottom of life, and how does one pick up what's left and move on from there?"

The months following her job loss were difficult, as she was not able to keep utilities turned on in her small rental home. Even her car was repossessed. One day, in the midst of a mighty pity party, she shouted out loud, "WHY?"

Her scream reeked of anger, defiance, aloneness, and hopelessness. Not really expecting any real answer, she began to list—still out loud and counting on her fingers—all the good things she'd done over the years and how this made her a good person. Why would all this wreckage come to her?

She jerked as she heard a voice answering her questions: "I Am the Lord your God, and you will not have other gods before Me." *WHAT?* Sue watched her cat, lying at her feet, bristle and lay back her ears. Something really had happened. Could God be talking to her?

Next, Sue heard, "The first and most important commandment is that you love Me above everything else; the second is that you love people as yourself."

For a few moments, the surroundings around Sue froze.

Stunned, she saw her past life flash through her mind. Everything in her life to this moment had been more important to her than God. She had spent her life worshiping earthly idols.

God's verbal answer to her confirmed He is real. Her faith had been abstract and outside of her, but now she knew profoundly that God cared *specifically* about her—Sue—and specifically chose her to be His and His alone. He had verbally called her, and this knowledge electrified her.

That was the turning point in her faith.

In coming to terms with her life and surrendering to her God, Sue found He is faithful. He constantly confirms His love for her. "God has peeled back layers of my sin nature and calls me *chosen*," she says, with tears in her eyes. She marvels that the Creator of the universe would love her enough to strip away her idols and draw her into His presence.

These days, Sue doesn't own a lot of material goods, but she is at peace and exceptionally blessed. "Now my service to others is not for my own edification, but is done in God's name, for His glory, and reaps benefits for God's kingdom. God has given me a voice to speak His name and a testimony to tell the world."

Having come through the darkness and been covered by the hand of God in it, Sue proclaims in the light all He has done for her: "I am chosen, blessed, adopted, forgiven, redeemed, and accepted. I am truly loved."

She adds, "The fire to do everything He places in my path is consuming and makes me want to be like Isaiah: 'I heard the voice of the Lord, saying: "Whom shall I send, and who will go for Us?" Then I said, "Here am I! Send me"'" (Isaiah 6:8).

The Way Forward

Where do you go to meet with God? Mrs. Job went to a lonely stone bench within a dried-up garden wall. Perhaps her spirit felt as dried up and colorless as the bench or the dead plants around it. Admitting deadness within us is the first step in approaching God. We come to Him with our empty hands and souls to await His filling.

Who can know the mind of God? When we come face-to-face with Him and all other things are stripped away, we fall on our knees before Him. God alone knows us thoroughly and directs the pathways of our lives. Our part is to humble ourselves and follow Him wherever He leads, surrendering our lives to His will, no matter what it looks like. He has the best plan for us.

In her writings, B. J. Hoff prayed:

> Remind me, Lord, when I would insist on having my way, that you bought all rights to my soul and my heart when you paid for my sin on the Cross.[8]

Meditation Questions

1. Have you expected only good from God?
2. What do you do when God disappoints you?
3. Do you despair when you mess up, thinking God is finished with you?
4. What stinks in your life? Is it a secret or an open sore? Will you dare today to lay it before God and let Him clean it up?
5. How can you keep short accounts with God and others?
6. After coming to terms with disappointment, or forgiving yourself and others, how might the way open for purpose and direction?

Journal Question

Journal about how God continues to work in your life, even after you have messed up. Tell your own story to yourself and ask

God for His forgiveness. What rebuke may need examination? Who might you need to forgive? Then look for God's hand in His purpose for you over time. Can you discover some directions in which He is leading you? Write down your insights.

Prayer

"Shall we indeed accept good from God, and shall we not accept adversity?" (Job 2:10).

Thank You, Lord, for loving us and caring about where our hearts choose to go. Please forgive our rage against You when life does not go as we wish. As adversity and tragedy strike our lives, show us Your strength, wisdom, and comfort. Let it be that we become victorious over those things that would destroy us. We trust in You. Thank You for Your kind restoration. We are blessed by Your love. Make us ready to move forward into Your purposes for us. So be it. Amen.

FOUR

Acceptance and Compassion

Blessed be the name of the LORD.
Job 1:21

It could have happened this way . . .

Mrs. Job's face tightened as she fought to control the tears in front of her husband. Nerve endings screamed all over her face in revolt. She could feel her muscles tighten up in the back of her neck.

Despair nearly overwhelmed her as she watched Job pick at his sores. She could see the silent agony he endured. His lips moved, and she knew he was talking to his God.

She poked at the fire and adjusted the pot on top that cooked their lunch. A bit of leek soup and grain for bread. She shook her head, remembering past feasts they had served to guests. What delicate dishes and fine goblets, and what delectable food and drink! How she missed it. Now, she was the only cook, and meals were—barely edible. She sent a final shove to the dung that fueled the fire. Dung!

She pulled four bowls from a makeshift cupboard. Next, she spooned the meager soup for her husband's meal, and for his three friends who had come to sit with him. He smiled wanly as he took it from her to drink. She passed along the bowls for the other men, and they nodded their thanks. After making sure all their needs were met, Mrs. Job leaned against the door, her arms folded, her back to the men inside. Her eyes closed against the dirty street and the dust that flew with every footstep hurrying past her mud house.

What would become of them? Of her? Her husband was so ill. What if he died? What would she do? A woman alone, where could she go? Would anyone help her? She'd been born into privilege. She'd learned to run a household—with servants to do her bidding. She had never given much thought to people outside her social circle. She had not contemplated how they lived.

Now "they" were her.

If ever things change, oh God, please help me to remember these days and be compassionate wherever I can.

She had quit praying that God would deliver her from this life. Sweeping, mending, and cooking were second nature these days. She had become expert at dressing her husband's sores and could do it without flinching. Daily, she rose from her mat, her ears now accustomed to Job scouring his skin. She barely registered the dust that filled her nose when she sniffed.

Footsteps stopped in front of her, and she opened her eyes. The servant of a former friend offered her a basket. She took it, and the servant stepped back, bowed his head, then turned away. She watched him walk up the street until she could see him no more. His clothes had not been ragged and dirty like hers. And he was a servant.

She sighed as she brought in the basket. She had no more room for snobbishness. Gratitude being uppermost, she delved in to see what her old friend had sent. Silent tears rolled down her cheeks as she pulled out wheat, beans, barley, onions, garlic, lettuce, still-warm bread, barley beer, and some dried meat! Once upon a time, she set her table with all cuts of meats. Now it seemed the Sabeans were enjoying her husband's animals. At the bottom she found healing supplies, especially salve for skin problems and strips of fabric for bandages.

Bless you, my friend.

She wiped her face, picked up the salve and bandages, and knelt before her husband, ignoring his three friends. He looked up and paused. Gently, she took his filthy hands into hers and kissed the palm of each hand. She summoned a smile for him and began to minister relief to his sores.

Meanwhile, in the book of Job . . .

After seven days of silence before Eliphaz, Zophar, and Bildad, Job's comforters, Job opened his mouth and began to lament. He began with cursing the day of his birth.

"May the day perish on which I was born. . . . Why is light given to a man whose way is hidden, and whom God has hedged in? For my sighing comes before I eat, and my groanings pour out like water. For the thing I greatly feared has come upon me, and what I dreaded has happened to me. I am not at ease, nor am I quiet; I have no rest, for trouble comes" (Job 3:3, 23–26).

Coming Alongside

Have you ever lamented that the thing you feared happened to you?

At times, I have had a faint idea of what it means to share in the fellowship of Christ's sufferings. I admit this has puzzled me. Didn't the sufferings of Jesus cover everything? He saved us from our sins. His blood flowed over Skull Hill, down through the valley, out through the portals of all time, inviting us to gather under the flow and be cleansed.

I'm discovering there is a sweetness in shared suffering. We can't stop the bad things that happen to us or our loved ones, but we can bring them to our Abba Daddy because Jesus made the way for us to do so. He invites us to come. We can also share our sufferings with one another.

During one of life's seasons, plenty of opportunities were presented for shared suffering: a friend lost motor functions in her body, and doctors scrambled to find reasons. We, her friends and family, stayed by her side to love, laugh, and pray together.

Another friend went on to heaven a short time later. But before she left, we had time to gather around her. We communicated to her our loving care and recounted our shared memories. When her time came to leave earth, we thought we lost her too soon. But only God knows our time frame.

At the same time, my own teenage grandson battled cancer; another friend's family got a diagnosis of cancer for their three-year-old. Still another family kept vigil by a mother whose fall caused a blow to her head and left her in a coma. All had faithful family and friends around them.

We often fear a trauma will happen. Sometimes it does, and lament arises from our souls. When the trauma is real, we need someone to come alongside us.

Perhaps there is purpose after all in sharing our sorrows as well as our joys. In doing so, we prove that we do indeed need one another. Somehow, in sharing our sorrows, they become a little more bearable.

Our God has never left us. He has not changed. His heart has always been to gather us under the safety of His wings, like the mother hen does her chicks (Matthew 23:37). He is our place of safety when the world whirs around us. He is strong. He knows our grief. He knows what we need at all times. He is faithful. He is trustworthy. He goes before us. He is our rear guard. His arms are around us. He offers His peace as we trust Him in our storms.

When life takes a side path, there is a time of adjustment, a time to digest events that led to this present time—a time to become accustomed to a new set of circumstances.

Job's friends came to sit with him for seven days in silence. At first, that's all they did. Since Mrs. Job had determined to be silent at first, too, it must have been eerily quiet. Maybe the sounds from beyond the dirt hut floated through the room. The shouts of people on the street could be heard, while animals shuffled by and stirred up the dust. Perhaps the swish of a broom and sounds of eating utensils slashed through the hush as Mrs. Job made meals from whatever edible scraps she could find.

In those days, a fall from social grace often could not be bridged. Though Mrs. Job may have had no friend to come to her side, she might have been grateful for a servant sent with a care basket full of food and other needed items. Perhaps she had not been forgotten.

After a time of silence, Job's friends listened quietly. They allowed him to vent his frustration, his anger, his fear. At this point, they sat in nonjudgment. Sometimes no words are available—or needed—to comfort one in great distress. But the presence of a friend can be like the presence of God.

Laments, Benches, and Whys

I once told myself that I could not ask God why questions. In my mind, to do so was a lack of faith in God's sovereignty. After all, He comprehends all things, and I should just trust Him.

I have changed my mind.

Why should my seventeen-year-old grandson be going through a very serious second bout with cancer? Why should my daughter go through breast cancer at the same time? Why should my mom go through cancer at this time too? Why should a young, healthy friend suddenly die of a heart attack? Why should a mind fail in a still-functioning body? Why should a three-year-old battle cancer or a six-year-old suffer with leukemia? Why must families be fragmented? Does God know, after all?

Yes, of course, the standard answer is that we live in a fallen world. We have inherited the sin of our first father and mother. All the earth and its inhabitants groan under the weight. But even recognizing this truth isn't enough for our despairing hearts.

Jeremiah asked God the why questions. Known as the weeping prophet, he shed tears over his homeland and people constantly for years. He wasn't afraid to ask God why—even going so far as to accuse God of not caring. He wrote the book of Lamentations, in which he shows us how to lament our pain and then turn to God with hope. Circumstances don't change, but the presence of God comforts us.

Mark Vroegop, in his book *Dark Clouds, Deep Mercy: Discovering the Grace of Lament,* gives us a glimpse of crying out to God in this way. He opens his book with a family tragedy and many anxieties to address. Recounting how he poured out his sorrow to God, Mark says, "I wrestled with sadness that bored a hole in my chest. In the midst of my pain, I began to find words and phrases in the Bible that captured the emotions of my heart. Some leapt off the pages. The Bible gave voice to my pain."[1]

Learning to lament in his heartache took Mark and his family on a very long journey. "Lament helped us navigate the wilderness of our grief."[2] He says, "Lament is how we bring our sorrow to God. Without lament we won't know how to process pain."[3] Finally, he invites us to join him on this journey: "There is deep mercy under dark clouds when we discover the grace of lament."[4]

David asked the why questions in the Psalms. He spent plenty of time running for his life and despondent that things would never be different. Over and over, he questions God while pouring out the agony of his heart. Hope would not let go.

> My God, my God, why have you
>   forsaken me?
> Why are you so far from saving
>   me,
>   so far from my cries of anguish?
> My God, I cry out by day, but you
>   do not answer,
>   by night, but I find no rest.
> Yet you are enthroned as the Holy
>   One;
>   you are the one Israel praises.
> In you our ancestors put their trust;
>   they trusted and you delivered
>   them.
> To you they cried out and were saved;
>   in you they trusted and were not
>   put to shame. (Psalm 22:1–5 NIV)

When Jesus was dying on the cross, He quoted this psalm. At that point, the forces of hell were dancing as Jesus cried out, "Why, Father?"

Father God heard Him. Two days later, Jesus rose from the dead to give us the greatest hope of all time: eternal reconciliation with Him and our loved ones. In Lamentations, Jeremiah proclaimed that God's mercies are new every morning. David's psalms—and most of all, Jesus's resurrection—are the proof of this. Hope is eternal.

How it must have squeezed Mrs. Job's heart to hear the laments of her husband. She could not stop his pain. She could apply salves to sores, but she could not cushion his emotional and mental suffering. To hear her beloved cry out his wish that he'd never been born must have ripped into the fabric of her own life.

His trouble was her trouble. His fear was her fear. If his groanings were pouring out like water, then so were hers.

Mrs. Job's story appears to indicate she had been thrust into the role of caregiver for her husband as his health deteriorated. Perhaps she had not been prepared to care for someone in that way. Did the chills of fear and panic race along her backbone? What if she was of no earthly good to him in his physical ailments? No servant stood in the doorway waiting for her call to come to his aid. She must do this herself. Perhaps she straightened her back with resolve. She loved her husband; she would care for his wounds.

When life throws us a big change like this, how can we understand what it will cost us? Insurmountable mountains of every kind stand before us. For some, it may mean, for a time, giving up their goals in life in order to minister to a loved one. Perhaps it means attending counseling sessions and working through emotional trauma. Others lose loved ones to disasters or disease. Only God is big enough.

Job's friends came alongside him. Mrs. Job must have served them all. Did she ever have help in her service? As her social position deteriorated, maybe her pride stopped her from asking for help. Or maybe it was not possible for her to ask for help. Perhaps she continued to run to the stone bench in the dusty park alone to sob out her grievances to God.

Supposing Mrs. Job's sympathetic socialite friend sent a basket in secrecy, it was a moment for relief and gratitude. But Mrs. Job yet may have been forced to accept social mores that prevented interaction. Repeatedly, she may have stumbled to the bench to struggle with bitterness.

If we believe that God's mercies toward us are new every morning, then we can know He listened to her compassionately. Sarah

Young, in *Jesus Calling*, gives us an idea of how God longs for us to come to Him with our worries and griefs. Speaking as if in the voice of Jesus, she writes:

> As My thoughts rise up within you, they become entangled in those sticky webs of worry. Thus, My voice is muffled, and you hear only "white noise."

> Do not be deafened by the noise of the world or that of your own thinking. Instead, *be transformed by the renewing of your mind.* Sit quietly in My Presence, letting My thoughts reprogram your thinking.[5]

As Mrs. Job sought to learn from her husband's rebuke, she may have battled to bring her initial rage under control and submit to the tutelage of circumstances. Back and forth, she grappled to know God. She may have mused about what He meant her to learn.

While she was seemingly alone at her stone bench, God met her there to soothe her broken heart. Mrs. Job learned to tame her emotions and sought the wisdom that came from a gentle, quiet spirit. Mrs. Job lamented her pain, rested from duty, and then regrouped in order to keep going.

God meets us at our benches. What a relief it is to know that we are not alone in our catastrophes. God is always present with us and empathizes with every blow that falls. His compassion is ceaseless. Remember—His mercies are new for us every morning. He is closer than a whisper away.

He works in places we don't see. While we may be showing one face to the world, God is working in the depths we don't reveal to anyone—even ourselves! He follows His own plan, even if it doesn't look so good to us at the time, and even when we must go to our knees in lament. He does His work in His way. We may not see the results we want, but His great design will be apparent at the right time—as He intended.

It's not up to us to fix it. We can't.

Our part is to cry out our sorrows before God, then to wait on answers in His time—to trust He will accomplish His purposes.

> Remember my affliction and roaming,
> The wormwood and the gall.
> My soul still remembers
> And sinks within me.
> This I recall to my mind,
> Therefore I have hope.
> Through the Lord's mercies we are not consumed,
> Because His compassions fail not.
> They are new every morning;
> Great is Your faithfulness. (Lamentations 3:19–23)

Change of Perspective

Mrs. Job wept at what would become of her and her husband. I have done that too. Doing so is fear based and forgets to take God into account. God always welcomes us back to Him. In our failings, He is consistent in His compassion and waits for us to return. He is faithful; His face is turned toward us.

Some days are so overwhelming that prayer seems impossible. Emotions swirl, thoughts get jumbled, and we can't sit still. I had such a day recently. It started in a funk that I simply could not pull myself out of. I knew God was close, but words for prayer would not come.

Sometimes a change of scenery helps, so I decided to get out of the house. After jumping into the car, I drove around in a drifting pattern until I was ready to receive from God. Slowly, He began to remind me of His constant love—even when I feel blown to bits or have just plain blown it. He loves me when I feel alone or depressed or out of sorts.

Father God is always faithful.

He drew me in from my aimless wandering that day. What could I discover from all I saw? I live by two rivers, and my roving usually takes me to the water. So much life revolves around the water, and here my senses are open to receive.

He impressed upon me to live in the moment. *Don't borrow trouble. Don't dwell on discord.* He admonished me to concentrate on the good, true, and noble. In doing this, I would be uplifted and not dragged down. I could choose my mood.

In the Bible, we are informed that if we bring everything to God in prayer, if we bring our requests to Him with thanksgiving, then He promises to guard our hearts and minds in peace. It is here you and I are encouraged to look forward in hope. "Whatever things are true, whatever things are noble, whatever things are just, whatever things are pure, whatever things are lovely, whatever things are of good report, if there is any virtue and if there is anything praiseworthy—meditate on these things" (Philippians 4:8).

The river always teems with life, and this day was no different. Its waters are constantly rolling and chasing, though it is sometimes calm on the surface. It changes with every light—morning, noon, and night. Wildlife draws sustenance from it. Fish swim their whole lives in it. People travel over it in all kinds of boats and floating vessels. As the river keeps moving in its direction, so does life. Always forward.

That evening, smoky skies magnified the setting sun. The brilliant red globe lowered in the dusk. Gold and green faded in the dusk over the tranquil river. A treasure of beauty. A treasure of peace. I felt restored.

It's marvelous that a simple jaunt can change your perspective.

Gail's Story

My friend, Gail, and I sometimes surprise each other at an overlook on the Spokane River. We attend different churches on Sundays, but occasionally our services dismiss around the same time, and we head for "our place."

My phone camera is always pointed toward the rushing water over the rocks below. Each season has its own expression and color. In the spring, we search for buttercups and take pictures of sunflowers. Summer brings new grasses blowing under a blazing sunshine on the hillside. The autumn blushes with color before it fades to the white of winter ice.

Gail and I both have an affinity for our river. It freshens our spirits and changes our perspectives at any season.

In finding the river as a place of refreshment, Gail has her own story.

Gail and Gary have served in full-time ministry all their married life. At times they worked in other countries, but eventually came back home to continue their service. They have raised two boys and enjoy their seven grandchildren.

Nevertheless, it has not always been smooth sailing. There was a time when Gail had no family nearby and needed someone to hold up her arms in the midst of the battle the way Aaron and Hur held up the arms of Moses to ensure victory for the Israelites in a long-ago battle.

Gail and Gary juggled responsibilities for several ministries. At one point, when their marriage struggled, they could not see the way before them. Gary's work took him out of town for one or two weeks each month, which left Gail alone with the children. The responsibilities of the ministries in which they assisted weighed heavily upon her as well.

During one of those weeks, tears welled up in Gail's eyes as she heard the news that he would be staying another week out of town. She walked down the path to her favorite place by the river.

"I can't do all of this, God. It's too much for me! I'm going under!" Gail cried, burying her head in her arms as she sat on steep wooden steps. Hidden near the underbrush by the water's edge, she spilled out her desperate prayers. Stately ponderosa pines stood sentinel above her, and the agitating waters rushed and swirled around the rocks as they hurried downstream, chasing spring runoff.

The river witnessed her tears. How would she manage all alone?

"Single parenting wasn't what I had in mind when I said, 'I do.' The boys need their dad—I need their dad! God, help me; I'm drowning!" Gail sobbed.

The clouds parted just long enough for a ray of sun to touch her shoulder. She raised her head to stare at the churning waters where something dark and bobbing caught her eye. A mallard popped up his blue-green head. Startled to see anything survive the muddy waters, Gail stood and immediately spoke comfort to the duck: "Poor baby, you're all alone too. And your life is so turbulent, like mine."

Gail slowly sat back down as she realized concern for this creature was unnecessary; the duck was confident and in his element, though she could drown in that icy water. A life preserver of truth had been thrown to her. She peered again through the barren branches, but the duck disappeared around a bend. Because of the watery chaos, she whispered a prayer of protection for her feathered friend.

Just as the clouds above had parted to let a shaft of light flow, the truth she had witnessed flooded like a sunbeam into her heart. God made ducks to survive quite nicely on water—smooth or rough. In the same manner, Gail was created for the course she currently traveled. It might be smooth or it might be rough, but with the help of the Holy Spirit, she would arrive at her destination too.

With a smile, Gail looked up through the tall pines and prayed. "Yes, Lord, You have given me everything to make this journey. Doubt and worry, you drown! Self-pity and fear, get off my shoulders and take a ride down the river! I *can* do this—no matter how muddy the waters and swift the current of life! Not by my strength, but with You, dear Jesus, I can do all things!"

Her heart buoyant, she climbed back up the bank where she could see beyond the bend in the river. She spotted the mallard, still confidently bobbing up and down through the next stretch of squally waters. Assurance of God's understanding guidance and help flooded her heart.

God is a tender Father. As Gail put herself in a place to receive, He provided one of His creatures to change her perspective and allowed her to move forward. He will provide whatever is needed for all of us who seek Him.

Gail and Gary have now celebrated forty-five years of marriage. At one time in the past, they doubted they could continue. But through hard work, determination, and faith in God's promises, they rebuilt their relationship. They have written a book together, *Better than Before*, with an accompanying workbook. They eagerly share what they have learned. As a pastoral couple, they have mentored other couples, taught marriage classes, and spoken at marriage retreats. They love to see marriages restored in faith.[6]

"Not by might, nor by power, but by my Spirit, says the Lord of hosts" (Zechariah 4:6 esv).

Community

"God knows the needs of his children, and he often works through us, prompting us to help one another. When we act on such promptings, we tread on holy ground, for we are allowed the opportunity to serve as an agent of God in answering a prayer." This wisdom comes from Kathleen H. Hughes.[7]

Staying tuned in to the promptings of God takes "bench time." Being given the opportunity to serve as God's answer to prayer is an awesome responsibility. It's a great gift—to us, as well as to those to whom He sends us.

Sometimes we get frustrated with our lack of words when things go wrong. It's okay. Job's friends came alongside him and said nothing for a week. He drew comfort from their silent support as they sat with him. Instead of staying away, understand the hardships in your community and trust God to give you what they need. Maybe they just need your silent presence with them. God has designed us for community; He will respond to your prayer.

At times, community may mean persistence. In *The Christmas Miracle of Jonathan Toomey*, Susan Wojciechowski tells a wonderful tale of persistent community.

The story is set in the post–Civil War era. A young widow and her son relocate after her husband perished in the war, and life goes from a gracious mansion to small-town rough living. In the process, the boy loses a carved nativity that he and his dad used to set up each Christmas Eve. Now Dad is gone, and so are the nativity figures. In the new surroundings, a wood-carver lived a little way out of town. He had lost his wife and child and lived a bitter life alone. He resisted every effort of the community to reach out to him.

The boy became fascinated with the creations of the wood-carver and asked if he would teach him to carve. At first the man refused, but the boy came back every day to ask again. Persistence.

Eventually, the boy and the wood-carver both overcame their depression when they created a new nativity together that told its old story to them.[8]

When we persist, we deal with our own pride, as well as the pride of others in this era of fierce independence. When someone is in a tough spot, we do want to help. But—what if the ones in need are *us*? What if we feel paralyzed by our situation? What do we do besides pace or stare at the wall?

Reach out. Ask for help. Lean on your community. Let loved

ones help—in prayer or practical ways. As you know they are pray-ing, you will feel their intercession undergirding you. If you can't pray and can't act, then you can be assured that God will make some provision for you.

It's okay to lean. The Holy Spirit's job is to come alongside, after all. He does it in your soul, of course, but most often, He inspires someone to come and help. So—lean.

Terri's Story

Going with the flow could best describe how Terri cared for her parents in their last years. When her dad's health failed and he went to heaven, her mother, Bobbi, was by his side. Bobbi's faithful at-tendance eased his last days for him and the family. Terri calls that time "a God thing."

Shortly after, it became apparent that Bobbi needed extra help herself. Terri began to oversee her mother's health care.

"It flowed like a progression. I began to stay the night at Mom's. Stairs got hard for her to navigate, and the laundry in the basement became a problem. It was a slow advance of needing more care. Mom never put expectations on my sister or me. She was always grateful for what we did."

In time, Bobbi needed more care. An electric wheelchair and other resources rolled along. Terri's sister Marilynn and friends stayed with Bobbi, allowing Terri to continue to take vacations around the world with her friend Angie.

Then Bobbi spent some time in the hospital after a fall. Terri noticed a profound change in her. Bobbi had always been feisty and determined with her own ideas of how things should work. But after her fall, that confidence slipped.

"I saw her become fearful and anxious as her health deteri-orated. My care for her increased. I found myself giving orders like, 'You need to get up,' and 'You need to eat.'" Terri pressed her mother to do things she was reluctant to do.

Another phase of health care began with the visiting nurses, and then hospice. After a consultation with the doctor, it was decided that Bobbi would stay home, in familiar surroundings, where she could be in her own bed at night. But things changed.

Their faith family and friends came alongside Terri and Marilynn. Frequently, someone came to either help Bobbi in some way or sit with her so Terri could have some time off.

Terri laughs as she tells about the time her mother's chair needed replacing. "Angie went with us, and we took Mom to the furniture store to get exactly the right chair. We made her sit in many of them. She did some grumbling, but we wanted to be sure she got a chair she would be comfortable in. We decided on one that would lift her up, and Mom seemed happy with it. We got the chair home; then she decided she didn't like it, and she wanted her old chair back. But the old chair had already gone to a charity."

Bobbi never wanted to be a burden. Health issues deepened, but so did the friendships. Those who came would listen to Bobbi's stories, watch TV, read with her, and enjoy visiting.

"I did pretty well," says Terri. "Sometimes I had some trouble sleeping, and sometimes I felt trapped. Then there was 'dirt therapy.' When I just had to get away yet be available if needed, I would head out to Mom's yard and garden. I planted, weeded, and cleared out flower beds. When I came back in, she was worried about where I'd been. But that dirt therapy calmed me through a few difficult moments."

Terri remembers when a group of ladies came to pray with her. They did not disturb her mom, who was napping in her room. They sat in the living room with Terri and prayed. She remembers that time being very comforting.

Friends kept coming.

The last six months, Bobbi was uncomfortable. "Mom had a goal. She wanted to go to heaven and not live to be one hundred years old as her father had." Terri chuckles as she recalls that determination of her mother's. She remembers a visit from Pastor Rod and Amy.

"So how are you doing, Bobbi?" Pastor Rod asked her.

"I'm really mad at God," she quipped.

"Why is that?"

"I want to go to heaven, and I'm still here!"

The time came when Bobbi got her wish. She slipped into eternity quietly and gracefully.

Terri's friend Jeanne sent a condolence card that arrived at the perfect right time when Terri was contemplating all the *should haves*. Encouragement flowed through her when she read, "Do NOT go to *I ought to haves*!"

Terri and Marilynn made the necessary arrangements. "I don't think I had a bad experience with anyone, medical or otherwise, during this time," Terri says thoughtfully. "My faith has grown through all of this."

Many of us struggle with the yokes put on our lives, but the afflictions we face don't need to drain us. When we don't have energy, someone may come alongside us to help us accomplish our lists, give us a needed change of perspective, send us encouragement, or pray with us. This is what community does—whether at church, a senior center, or somewhere else. We don't walk alone.

Once again, it's okay to lean. This is what the Holy Spirit waits for us to do, and then He steadies us.

After Bobbi went to heaven, Terri wrote a note to her Garland Church family:

> I'm listening to "By Our Love" by the group For King and Country as I write this.
>
> Dear Garland Family, you will never know how much I love and appreciate you. I could not have cared for my parents these past years without your help in a variety

of ways: you've prayed for us; listened to me and given wise advice; visited; read to my mom; called to remind Mom about Gonzaga games; celebrated holidays with us; and provided physical, emotional, and spiritual care. You are truly the best and most caring family ever! Never let anyone tell you anything different.

Purpose

Winston Churchill once said, "Never give up. Never give up. Never, never, NEVER give up!" What good advice! The Bible says the same thing—not to grow weary in well-doing (2 Thessalonians 3:13).

We live in obscurity, mostly ignorant of God's purposes for us. Life is so noisy. Social media claims so much of our attention. If it isn't that, then the news keeps us tottering on our toes. It seems that with every change of life we forget there is one purpose to keep us on track: doing the will of God. Yet we struggle with wondering what God wants us to do. Which direction does He want us to go? Will our current chosen path glorify God?

Often, we are afraid to change direction. But who can tell if God's purpose means us to do exactly that? What if God sees great potential in us? What if He is constantly calling us to be available for His purposes?

I am inspired by the story of Gideon in the book of Judges. God had a purpose for Gideon, but he lived in obscurity.

His story begins as God calls out to him while he is threshing wheat in the winepress. An unlikely place to do it, but the wheat needed to be hidden from the enemies of Gideon's time, the Midianites, who were marauding the countryside.

I imagine how this call of God went.

"The Lord is with you, oh mighty man of valor"—mighty hero."

Possibly Gideon looked up in amazement to view the man who

had suddenly appeared, whereupon a conversation ensued—the kind of chat we always want to have with the Lord instead of listening to what He has in mind for us. "If God is with us, then why is all this bad stuff happening?" we ask repeatedly today.

But once they got past that discussion, God told Gideon that He wanted him to lead an army against the Midianites. God wanted to give Israel freedom in victory.

Gideon might have abandoned the wheat and stood before the man. Looking this way, then that way, he denied he could do such a thing as lead an army. "I can't do that!"

The Scriptures record this as, "Oh my Lord, how can I save Israel? Indeed, my clan is the weakest in Manasseh, and I am the least in my father's house." Perhaps his knees were knocking. Being from the weakest clan certainly sounded like a good excuse.

"Surely I will be with you, and you shall defeat the Midianites as one man." The Lord then reassured Gideon that he was the "man of the hour."

What? A simple farmer threshing his wheat, minding his own business? A simple farmer in hiding too! Hardly a mighty warrior! But God called out the potential in this man to serve His purposes.

At that point, Gideon requested the Lord to wait while he prepared a sacrifice. The Lord graciously waited. After the offering, the Lord set it afire and disappeared.

After receiving such assurance, a fiery miracle that should have sealed the deal, Gideon requested more signs. Perhaps he wanted to make sure. The Lord patiently fulfilled every request.

Isn't that just like us? "Why would God choose an obscure nobody like me?" We know ourselves to be sinners and unworthy of great heavenly missions.

But God *does* choose us. Not only does He choose us, but He sees who He made us to be, not who we see ourselves to be. Is that not love? Is that not purpose?

We are made in the image of God, with potential to do remarkable things He has designed us to do—to create. It's wonderful to know He loves us in such a way. He equips us for those grand deeds.

We need to say yes when He calls us. What would it be like to be called a mighty warrior by God?

"The Lord is with you, you mighty man of valor" (Judges 6:12).

Not Interruption, but Opportunity

I used to get downright disgusted when my plan for the day got kinked up. I always checked my day planner several times to make sure I could check items off my list. At the end of the day, success meant that I'd accomplished every task I'd scheduled for the day.

The problem was that people kept interfering with my list. Such an annoyance!

As we rush headlong through life with our electronic planners in hand, what might we miss? Maybe an eagle sitting in a tree above, a couple of deer racing across the street, or a line of quail scurrying alongside the road.

Perhaps it's something more important, like stopping to help someone in need on our way to where we're going. It may make us late to a weighty meeting, but it could be that God planned this encounter. What might be the result?

Maybe it's the news of a serious illness for you or a family member. That disrupts a schedule quickly.

Maybe it's a missed deadline.

I am task oriented. I rush through the projects meant for each day. Over the years (yes, years), after repeating the same frustrations, I finally got it through my head that the intrusions into my day are not interruptions at all.

Instead, they are opportunities woven into God's plan for my life to make me into His image. Sometimes, the very interruption provides an opportunity to take a different path into something greater than I would plan for myself—even if that plan makes no sense to me. God directs our steps, and He may take us on a route we would rather not go, but His purpose for us is to make us a people in His image.

As we look in from outside the story, it seems that the life of Jesus was cruelly interrupted while He was in the prime of His life. But God, through Jesus's death and resurrection, made an opportunity for us to believe. When we believe in the Savior sent for us, we gain eternal life. Forever life would not be possible for us without Jesus allowing His life to be interrupted for our sakes.

Like Gideon, the circumstances of my life claim all my attention. I'm hiding from whatever may be out there to get in the way of the task in front of me. But if I raise my face, maybe I will find an angel of God calling my name in the form of an unwanted interruption. Maybe I will discover that God has a different plan for me, an opportunity with a greater purpose.

Is that not true for you too?

Life circumstances can dictate our emotions. Years ago, my husband struggled with drugs, alcohol, and mental demons. My life was interrupted by chaos. It was like trying to keep my head above water as my body swirled toward a vortex, ready to drag me down into a terrifying obscurity. When my husband overdosed and passed away, I was left to sift through the emotions of years.

Who is in charge? When a situation goes haywire on you, it's no surprise to God. Nothing comes to us unless it first passes through the hand of God. We might wonder how in the world a seriously awful situation can possibly be for our good. But God knows. He is, after all, building masterpieces in us. He is conforming us into His image, teaching us to trust Him.

God has our good in mind—always. Our interruptions are His opportunities given for us to grow in Him. His sights are set on a greater purpose for our lives than our own choices would provide.

He will be with us in every step we take, and because He is our Father, He is proud of those steps.

He promises never to leave us or forsake us. In every unexpected path. No matter what.

"A [woman's] heart plans [her] way; but the Lord directs [her] steps" (Proverbs 16:9).

Karen's Story

Mark's birth did not go smoothly.

Karen and Gary, her husband, had driven twenty-five miles from home to the hospital to induce Karen. They'd prayed it would be the right decision, but the distance between home and hospital made it practical. Lori, their three-and-a-half-year-old daughter, was left home with a family member. She was very excited about a new brother or sister.

A series of mishaps manifested throughout the day. The first came in the form of the medication used to induce Karen's labor. (It was pulled off the market two months later.)

"The first injection did not start the process, so they gave me a second," Karen says. Labor came too hard and fast. Karen could barely catch her breath as waves of pain rolled through her. "They gave me muscle relaxers to counter it. Mark was born in forty-five minutes."

No baby monitor had been available to discern if Mark had been in distress. "I saw him born through the mirror above me. When I first saw Mark, he looked perfect, but his color was kind of purple, and he wasn't breathing."

It took three minutes for Mark's first breath. The oxygen mask they clamped on his newborn face was adult sized. Karen sensed no panic or urgency as the medical team cared for her and her newborn. "I was calm. I'm not sure to this day whether it was due to shock or God protecting me."

Mark was whisked off to another room, but this hospital had no intensive care unit for infants, and the doctor who delivered him explained that the baby would be transported to another hospital that had a children's care unit.

No alarms were raised for them until they found out at the children's hospital that Mark had endured several seizures the first day of his life. Six days later he was released.

"The doctor said Mark would have some residual effects, maybe some learning disability. We were left with the idea that it was not serious," Karen remembers, with tears in her eyes. "We took him home, and I bonded with him when I nursed him. But he was unable to suck on a bottle. We learned later that it was a sign of a neurological problem."

At four months, Mark was not focusing, nor were there smiles or any interaction as Karen would talk to him. Remembering her daughter's normal development at the same age, Karen asked the doctor if there was a problem.

"He told me I was overreacting like a nervous parent!"

But at eleven months, the doctor informed Karen that Mark was severely developmentally delayed. He was not sitting up, crawling, or moving around much on his own. This began years of treatments and long days of Karen searching for help. Mark would not mature beyond a four-month-old infant. His care would be intense and would require teams of caregivers who would be going in and out of Karen and Gary's home constantly.

"People told me at the time that if I had enough faith, my son would be healed. Someone else asked me what I needed to learn from this situation. I went into a crisis of faith. I always thought that if I did the 'right' thing, bad things would not happen to me." Karen's bewilderment overwhelmed her.

Two years later, nearly to the day of Mark's birth, Marie was born. Karen and Gary were terrified throughout the birth process. They made sure monitors were used to gauge her progress. Then, as Marie began to develop normally, they rejoiced with every milestone she achieved. "It helped to give us some joy in the midst of the devastating sorrow we faced every day with our only son."

When Mark was four years old, litigation brought the family some financial help for his special needs. As Mark grew, he experienced health issues and hospitalizations. Early on, Karen was mainly responsible for his care, and caregivers were added. The family missed church often, as there was no provision for their special needs at church.

"I wrestled with my faith and wondered what good could ever come from our circumstances," Karen cried.

When Mark was twelve, it was time to find a group home for him. As a mother, Karen's heart wrenched at the thought of such a separation from her child, yet she could not continue to care for him and raise her daughters with their normal needs—so Mark was moved.

"I carried suitcases in my car and constantly wanted to bring him back home because they weren't caring for him as I would. But I had to realize I could not give him a perfect life any more than I could do that for my daughters."

Karen's girls are grown and live their own lives. Mark is still in his group home. Karen now lives on her own as well. She hasn't figured everything out, but she is coming to grips with God being present in her life no matter what. Because of the unexpected path God led her through, Karen has opportunities to care for others with compassion. She would have missed this gift had she not experienced the depths of sorrow she survived in caring for her disabled son.

Karen's desire is to honor her son's life in telling his story. His life has purpose.

> Therefore, since we have been justified through faith,
> we have peace with God through our Lord Jesus Christ,

through whom we have gained access by faith into this grace in which we now stand. And we boast in the hope of the glory of God. Not only so, but we also glory in our sufferings, because we know that suffering produces perseverance; perseverance, character; and character, hope. And hope does not put us to shame, because God's love has been poured out into our hearts through the Holy Spirit, who has been given to us. (Romans 5:1–5 NIV)

Karen knows the truth of the progression of perseverance, character, and hope. She believes hope keeps us going, and God continues to pour His love into us through the Holy Spirit.

Karen is like Gideon. When she was weak, God named her a warrior. Little by little, He gave her weapons to fight for her son and daughters. It was not what she would have planned for her life, but God has His own plans for us to be conformed into His image. The circumstances in our lives prepare us for this purpose.

Treasure

Do you create? If you consider yourself an artist, how do you view what you have made? When I create something, I usually treasure it because it's uniquely mine. It's special. I spend time considering shape, color, word selections, presentation, usefulness, or other aspects. I want it to be something great because I have put my time, talents, and effort into it.

It would be strange, indeed, if an artist created a beautiful painting and then walked away to leave it to its fate. We all love what we have created. We are proud of it. We treasure it. We don't just toss it somewhere.

If you had fashioned something that made you proud, what would it be like if someone trashed it? Suppose it was somehow spoiled and didn't live up to the objectives you intended for it. Would you pull out all the stops to fix it, or would you walk away, separate yourself from what you had made, and let the chips fall where they may? Wouldn't you make every effort to redeem what was broken?

A common notion floats in our globe that God is aloof and apart from this world He created. What a crazy idea, yet people think it all the time. If we are made in God's image, then God could no more walk away from us, His handiwork, than we can walk away from our own inventions.

Jesus came to show us that the Father's heart cares for us. He walked and talked with His creations. He came to stop evil, to re-possess His own belongings from the thief who stole and tarnished what God had called good.

Like us, God was proud of what He had made. We are all unique. He is intimately interested in the development of every one of us. Why else would He go to such lengths throughout history to claim us back?

We are His treasures.

"Then God saw everything that He had made, and indeed it was very good" (Genesis 1:31).

Meditation Questions

1. When you need to meet God and regroup, where do you go for a "bench break"?
2. Can you be satisfied with leaving the whys in the hands of God?
3. How have you supported someone else in their suffering?
4. What do you do to change your surroundings to help your attitude?
5. Do you allow your community to come around you to help in tough times?

6. Have you asked God to show you the purpose He has for your life?

7. How have the interruptions in your life become opportunities from God to grow?

Journal Question

Look for treasures from God in day-to-day living. List them and why you see them as treasures from God. How do these things speak of His love and care for you?

Prayer

"Blessed be the name of the Lord" (Job 1:21).

Jesus, let us learn to bless Your Name no matter what circumstances we find ourselves living. Let us praise You. Let us fix our eyes upon what You are working out in our lives. Help us to see the interruptions in life as ordained by You. Let us lean on our community. Let us see the treasures You are building in us and around us. May Your love conquer all our doubts and set us free. Amen.

FIVE

Silence and Listening

Though He slay me, yet will I trust Him.
Job 13:15

It could have happened this way . . .

The voice of Zophar, Job's friend, cut across the silence, nearly causing Mrs. Job to stab her finger with her mending needle. Zophar unfolded his legs underneath him and used his hands to shift his body more comfortably on the mat.

"You have said your heart is pure, Job, but if you would just prepare your heart, strengthen your hands, and ask Him to forgive you, He will. Then you could be steadfast once again, not afraid or miserable—and return to your position of respect in the city."

Hurt flashed across Job's face.

But before he could respond, Eliphaz, spoke up. "Job, you must learn to curb your tongue, for it testifies against you. Pretty speeches don't get you anywhere. God is not fooled. Beware of wickedness and seek wisdom." He nodded sagely, as if he had delivered some great insight.

Mrs. Job read a temper, quickly masked, on her husband's face. "No doubt you are perfect and enjoy great wisdom," he replied, "but I have understanding as well, and I am not inferior to you. I have called on God. I know He holds all things, and I await His answers. But now I am mocked by my friends."

Bravo! Mrs. Job silently cheered.

But they were not finished. Bildad spoke next. After cataloging the disasters that had befallen Job, he said, "It's difficult for a man to be righteous before God. The light of the wicked goes out so quickly, and his strength is shortened. I am sorry, Job."

At this, Job's eyes flashed. He made a careful show of scratching his forearms. "How long will you break me in pieces with your words? I will cry out to God and bring my case before Him!"

Everyone fell into an uncomfortable silence at this. The sun's rays through the door seemed to shift as dust motes danced in the air.

Mrs. Job sat quietly. She schooled her features and moved serenely through her mending as she listened to her husband's so-called comforters. But she couldn't stop her hands from shaking, and that made it hard to jab the needle into the material. She couldn't work one stitch, let alone mend the garment.

How DARE they lecture her man after the many kindnesses he had extended to them over the years! Did they think their words were *helping*?

No one was more devoted to his God than her Job.

She wanted to jump up and scream at them to *shut up*! She wanted to shout at them to *go away*!

"But God, why don't You do something to stop them? I can see their words offend him."

Listen to My voice. Job is a man of faith. He trusts in Me. I want this for you too. Will you trust Me to deal with them in due time?

My child, I will never leave you nor forsake you. Lay down your cares before Me, and watch Me work.

Tears ran down her face. Mrs. Job stilled, regaining her calm. Her heart eased from the rage.

She could rest and wait on God's time.

Meanwhile, in the book of Job . . .

Job didn't keep quiet. He responded to his friends. He told them in no uncertain terms that he already knew the things of which they spoke.

"I am not inferior to you," he insisted. He demanded an audience with God and called his friends' reasoning worthless to him. He continued to admonish them not to speak things about God of which they were ignorant. Good for Job! It must have been a balm to Mrs. Job's heart as she listened to this discussion.

Job's comforters had plenty of opinions. The book of Job is full of them. Perhaps it's because we, as humans, are driven to find the reasons behind whatever experiences happen to us. But it may be that we will never discern those reasons this side of heaven. This was true for Job. When God met him near the end of his story, God did not give Job any reasons why. Instead, God asked Job if he had the mind of God, and He threw unsearchable secrets at Job. In the end, Job could only humble himself before his God.

Yet we keep digging for reasons.

If only we could rest in the sovereignty of God, as Job learned to do, with the trust that He knows all things! It's not necessary that we know. But that sticks in our craw. We want to understand why.

Right Listening

Perhaps Mrs. Job considered shouting at her husband's friends, but clamped her lips shut lest she be accused once again of speaking like a foolish woman. Have you ever had such a reaction? What courage it must have taken to keep quiet when everything in her longed to defend her husband. When is it right to speak? When is it better to listen?

How do you respond when a disaster comes into your life, and then someone comes along and tries to explain it away in negative or disparaging terms? Maybe you reject their comments or advice and will them to go away—the sooner the better.

The Bible calls true wisdom the ability to listen to the words of God. As we seek such wisdom, we learn to deliberately put our minds on true, noble, and virtuous things. It's a choice to think this way. God promises to look after those who seek His wisdom.

"But whoever listens to me will dwell safely, and will be secure, without fear of evil" (Proverbs 1:33).

Control over your words gives you assurance. Just as Mrs. Job contained her words as she seethed with anger toward her husband's friends, making the choice to listen and control your own tongue avoids painful missteps and regrets.

Evidence of the devil's work is universal. If we look at his challenges to God over Job, we must assume all of us are targets. If we are beloved of God—and His Word assures us that we are—then it's only a matter of time before we will face a battle.

As we consider right listening, clearing our minds of emotions and thoughts that would pull us down the wrong road is essential. God has given His words to us to replace the wrong with the right. Scriptures urge us to withstand the wiles of the devil. It takes courage to stand firm. It takes strength to fight. We need our spiritual armor for protection.

Determining to live for God and grow in knowledge with holiness guarantees the inevitability of spiritual warfare. Fiery arrows shot at our thoughts and emotions stir us up, but God has provided spiritual armor and weaponry. The words of Scripture in Ephesians chapter 6 give us a sword. In addition, we are given the helmet of salvation, the shield of faith, and truth wrapped around us, along with shoes of good news for our defense.

What does this have to do with right listening? With the power of the Holy Spirit, we have control over our ears and our thoughts. We can stand firm and deny entrance to the whispers of the devil and his intent to destroy our lives.

When we resist, the devil flees. God's Word says so.

Finally, only time with God will open our spiritual ears. He longs for time with us.

Sometimes I hear a refrain sung by Larnelle Harris—"I Miss My Time with You."[1] It reverberates through my mind every time I hear it—for days, for longer.

I hurry through the busy day, having only done a short devotional that morning, but not really sitting with my Lover God. When do we share what's on our minds and hearts with Him?

There are no real uninterrupted blocks of time in our days unless we make that appointment—then keep it.

Do you ever hear His voice asking, "Do you miss your time with Me?"

I have. The tears well up in my eyes. Does my Lord have to ask me that?

"Yes, Lord, I do, but what about . . ."

It seems He *does* have to ask me that.

No excuses are good enough for not sitting down with the one who loves me, who wants to give me rest and peace and share His life with me.

I don't want us to miss our time together.

I want His voice to grow louder, to cover the din of my life. Let me choose Him first! Let the urgent tasks screaming at me fade away as I seek my time with Him. His voice remains soft and sweet, wooing me to listen to Him. To seek His eyes as they gaze longingly at me. Inviting me to come sit with Him. Drawing me closer. At the appointed time. So we don't miss our time together.

"As the Father loved Me, I also have loved you; abide in My love" (John 15:9).

Author Frances J. Roberts gives us insight in learning to listen rightly. Speaking as if in the voice of Jesus, she writes:

> When you pray, My child, do not make it a one-way conversation. Know I am listening, but know also I will respond and will speak to you if you give Me opportunity. Prayer is not only of the lips, but of the ear also, for prayer is of the heart, and the heart that has learned to love has learned to listen more than to speak!
>
> . . . When you come to Me in prayer, you ought to come to enjoy Me, not to entertain Me.[2]

Growth in Listening

As we journey with Mrs. Job, we marvel at her growth. We met her in the beginning as a pampered society wife who was completely unprepared for the disaster that disrupted her life. We witnessed her temper, her blame of God, and her impatience with her husband—even to the point of insulting him and his God.

Perhaps she never wondered about God. I wonder if Job prayed for her daily to come to know the one who held all things in His hands.

Many of us pray for spouses, children, and other loved ones to come to know Jesus. Does God hear those prayers? Yes, He is listening to us. Sometimes the answers may come in ways we can't fathom. Did it take destruction for God to answer Job's prayers for his wife? Perhaps she could have been reached in a less terrible way, but it is often big events that get our attention.

Job also wanted vindication before his doubtful friends. How dare they insinuate he was at fault! He knew he lived his life before God with as clear a conscience as possible.

Did the devastation Job endured open questions in his soul that he had not perceived were there? In the latter chapters of the biblical book, Job is given his wish: a confrontation with God. Job desperately wants to throw his why questions at God and demand answers.

What happened? Simply—Job listened.

God asked if Job was present when the foundations of the earth were formed. Of course he wasn't. Did Job know how God commanded the seas to adhere to boundaries? No, he did not. Did Job know how snowflakes were formed, making each one different? Well, no.

Before God was done interrogating Job, the mere man could only humble himself before God in worship. Did he know about all the things on earth that God had created? No, but he had come to understand that God is sovereign. God is Creator. God set all things in motion—even Job's life—and the universe acts accordingly.

The Bible doesn't say whether Mrs. Job heard any of this, but as her husband returned from his meeting with God, there must have been some interesting communication between them.

We have followed Mrs. Job from disbelief to rage, from rage to fear, and then from fear to repentance and acceptance. In the vignette in this chapter, we see her sitting, quietly listening, all the while growing indignant over how unkind and obtuse her husband's friends were to him. Yet she sat still and waited for God to speak to her heart. She learned He would care for her as well as for her husband.

I am amazed at how God talks to each one of us, even if we have never listened for His voice or recognized it. God gets across what He wants us to learn. Our God is about the business of growing our spirits and outfitting us to live in foreverland.

Connie's Story

"Looking back, I see God's fingerprints all over my life, working things out for my good," says Connie, a graceful woman of God.

She did not grow up with instruction about God. Her life has been a journey of learning.

When her husband, Jim, fell ill, life unraveled for Connie and her family. She remembers clearly hearing a voice telling her that Jim was going to die.

"It was an audible voice. I never heard it before that, and I've never heard it since," Connie explains. "But I knew it was God."

To her shock, Jim did die. Connie was left to raise her twelve-year-old son, Jeff. Because of that experience of hearing God's voice, she took small faith steps. However, the busyness of her life choked out her attempts.

"I didn't have the discipline it took to grow because I simply didn't have the time." Even so, Connie says the seeds were planted for the process of faith to grow when the season was ripe.

Jim's family invited Connie and Jeff to leave Colorado to join them permanently in Spokane, Washington. They moved. This proved to be a turning point for Connie.

Louise lived across the street from Connie and Jeff's new home. She welcomed them warmly, and they became close friends. Connie knew God had begun a pursuit of her. Connie drove Louise to church, and Louise invited Connie to Bible Study Fellowship. Connie soaked in wisdom from BSF, and Louise became her mentor.

Connie says, "I know my friendship with Louise is why God moved us across the street from her."

Louise's quiet faith spoke loudly to Connie. She gave Connie an example to follow.

"I saw that she loved God. This spoke to me about desiring

deeper levels of knowing Him," Connie reflected. "I gave my life to Jesus in Colorado, but that was just the seed. My faith blossomed when I met Louise and saw how she lived her life always listening to God. I wanted that."

Louise modeled following God in the light of His words: "Trust in the Lord with all your heart, and lean not on your own understanding; in all your ways acknowledge Him, and He shall direct your paths" (Proverbs 3:5–6).

When she passed away, Louise left Connie with a legacy of faith. Even now, Connie's face softens with remembered affection for her friend. She says, "Without those saints to show the way, there is no foundation."

Jeff grew up and moved out, and Connie was alone with time to listen. To her delight, her relationship with Jesus grew. "I came to a place of wanting Him, desiring His presence daily."

At BSF, Connie made other friends. Terri, a nurse, inspired Connie to go to nursing school where she got her degree and then started a new job. Everything changed for her once again. Her life gained order.

Through her circumstances, Connie began to understand her relationship with God better. She learned that faith is not about rules, but about Jesus. In her alone times at home, she yearned to experience His presence better. She fine-tuned her spiritual ears to listen for Him. She anticipated His company with excitement, and she welcomed Him.

"I call this God's reckless love. I was a reckless, angry person. I had issues. But God pursued me right through it. He never gave up on me. When I needed help, He brought people to me. When I needed Him in the quiet, His presence hovered over me." As she finishes her story, she smiles, with a light in her eyes: "I know He's there now in all the deep places."

God showed up for Connie many times in her life. She has come to believe in the promise of His goodness: "And we know that all things work together for good to those who love God, to those who are the called according to His purpose" (Romans 8:28).

When Connie thought of her own shattered dreams, she considered Naomi's story from the book of Ruth in the Old Testament.

Naomi was a bitter, angry woman who had nothing to live for. She dwelled in Moab, a foreign land. A famine had swept through Israel, her country. Naomi's family had traveled to a more prosperous land to escape the scarcity and loss. Ironically, it was in Moab where she really lost everything. Her husband and two sons died. She despaired of life. But God never left her. He had other plans. He gave Ruth, her daughter-in-law, as her companion. Ruth went home to Israel with Naomi, where she served the older woman and got to know the one true God. Eventually, Ruth married Boaz and presented Naomi with a grandson, who turned out to be in the line of the Messiah to come.

God took a bitter, angry, shattered woman and renewed her life and gave her joy!

There was a time when Connie would have railed at God through her pain and shattered dreams, but the shattered dreams are where she learned the most. In the deep silence, she had to learn to listen for God's voice.

She has learned to trust Him when pain happens. When she doesn't understand, He knows the rest of the story. She smiles.

"And—I'm not God. He is."

Listening with Insight

Have you heard this inner voice?

When you get too busy, I step back and wait until you are ready for relationship again.

How does it feel when God steps back and waits for you to remember Him?

I hear Him calling me back from somewhere else all too often.

I am not a person to sit around—ever. The mantra of my life is: "Wanna do everything; wanna see everything." Life is just too short to let it slide by. The result of this inner drive is constant motion—and sometimes energy dissipation.

But in my headlong race through life, I forget the most important thing: spending time with the one who loves me most and empowers my life. When I hear that inner voice, it stops me like sticky stuff on a smooth surface. Yeah—face-plant.

How do we start this listening with insight? *Sit in peace,* advises the inner voice. *Spend quiet time with Me. Listen to My voice. Read My Word for you today. I am waiting for you. I still miss My time with you.*

"God is waiting for *me*?" you might ask. Yes. He waits for us to realize we need silence to hear Him. We are a noisy people. Media options are usually blaring everywhere. Our schedules cause us to run between appointments and meetings. In order to hear God speaking to us, we must allow silence.

We don't sit still very well either. Stillness means rest, relaxation, ease, calmness, and leisure. How does it feel to think Jesus is already in stillness, waiting for you to join Him?

With sitting still comes the opportunity to reflect. In the quiet, introspection reveals the goodness of God, how patient and kind He is to wait on us. It is a time for grace.

Prayer is the communication between God and us. It's always open where God is concerned. He is ready to listen, then to speak to us. How easily we forget the one who longs to hear about our day.

Do you get silence from God when you pray? I suppose most of us do at times. However, prayer is our communication avenue to God. Through prayer, healing happens, evil schemes are broken, prophecies are heard, and much more.

But what if silence is the most profound communication God

has with us? Suppose the most intimate moments with God are those spent in silence. If that's so, how are we to understand?

I have heard it said that God's silence during our prayer with Him could be interpreted as deep listening.

Hold that thought. *Deep listening?*

Sometimes I sit on my porch to stare across the valley at the distant mountains. They look blue, varying hues according to distance. The blue sky (in the good weather months) is full of soft, cushy, pillow-like clouds.

A soft breeze soughs through the trees as I watch butterflies chase each other in circles above the lawn as the bushes gently sway.

It's quiet. I feel the presence of God deep in my soul. It's a place of rest and assurance. I sense that this is the quiet confidence of which the Scriptures speak.

Picture a child on her knees, elbows propped on Abba Daddy's lap, hands held together in a pose of prayer in front of her face. Abba Daddy is leaning over, His hand stroking the child's head. Listening. Hearing her heart. Hearing her words, yes, but mostly listening to her heart.

How do you feel when you have been heard?

Maybe that's how we should come away from a time of silent prayer.

Listening. That which we strive for but don't do well. But our Abba Daddy has all the time in the world to listen to us. I think He welcomes us into His lap and inclines His ear toward us. I wonder that our ears aren't much attuned to what He might be saying to us.

Do we really believe in His love for us? Yes, of course we know He made a way for us to be with Him for eternity. We accept His sacrifice for us. We count on what Jesus did on the cross and at His resurrection to save us. We can truly believe that the Lover of our souls is waiting for us. Every day.

To think that He rejoices over us with singing! Wow! We may

not feel we are worth it, but our God holds us as precious in His sight.

"The Lord your God in your midst, the Mighty One, will save; He will rejoice over you with gladness, He will quiet you with His love, He will rejoice over you with singing" (Zephaniah 3:17).

Silence in Listening

Have you been to a silent retreat? How hard was it to *not* talk? Did you wonder how you would fill the time?

It's not easy to spend a few days without speaking. Our phones, tablets, and other media outlets scream information to our minds relentlessly. We hardly have time for anything other than cursory thoughts.

If we are to practice the silence of deep listening, it takes a concentrated effort in our noisy era to plan for the time to sit and make it happen. God waits for us. I've heard it said that He is a gentleman. He invites, but never forces His way into our lives. We must open ourselves to Him and, in turn, invite Him to come.

Imagine yourself quietly wandering in a garden. Feel your senses come alive. The buzz of bees goes by your ears, and you watch them land on a luscious blossom to harvest its nectar. Hummingbirds pause to get a drink at a birdbath, their wings whirring. Perhaps the bushes rustle with a nameless critter hiding. Imagine the warmth of the sunshine caressing your skin.

Under the shade of a willow tree, in the middle of the fragrant garden, maybe a bench beckons. The relaxed branches sway in a slight breeze. You sit and let a sigh of contentment escape you.

With the words of God written in the Bible on your lap, peace seeps into your soul. You are ready to listen. When the way is clear and unfettered, God's voice can be heard in the depths of your heart. Close companionship with God is possible.

But perhaps you don't have access to a warm, sunny garden.

That's okay. Turn off the media around you and go to a quiet place. It takes planning and effort to make it happen, but God will meet you there.

All He asks for is time. We jealously guard our time because of so many demands upon it, but only we can set aside moments to listen. He does not do it for us.

Ruth Haley Barton, in her book *Invitation to Solitude and Silence*, says this, "The invitation to solitude and silence is just that. It is an invitation to enter more deeply into the intimacy of relationship with the One who waits just outside the noise and busyness of our lives. It is an invitation to communication and communion with the One who is always present even when our awareness has been dulled by distraction."[3]

She talks about our living in the chaos of life. We want to excel at our jobs, we volunteer at church, and we juggle the needs of our families, but how do we address the desperate longings in our hearts—if we can find the time to identify them?

Perhaps circumstances maneuver us to the place of silent seeking. God is waiting for us at that place.

Ruth Haley Barton admits it took her a year to be able to sit quietly before God. Her life kept her running; deadlines don't wait. Nor do dishes or laundry or soccer practice. Sitting still and being quiet doesn't accomplish anything—or does it?

As I have already explained, my life is one long rush. As a result, I am taking up the challenge of sitting quietly before God every day. I understand what Ruth wrote; all the to-do lists pop up abundantly in my mind. Last night, I sat on my porch with my hands in my lap for five minutes. My book and my phone were out of reach—on purpose. Instead, I heard the birdsong and watched a sunset. As the trees turned gold one by one, I wondered if this was the cool of the day when God once walked with Adam and Eve in the garden.

I have only just begun this journey. A battle for the mind will commence, I am sure, as Ruth warned. But I intend to go forward. It will be worth it to find that place of deep listening and companionship with Jesus. I will know I have been heard by the one who understands me best.

Ruth says we will not necessarily have words in our minds, but we will have the sense of God's presence with us.

Another way to listen is through a method called Lectio Divina. An ancient practice handed down to us from the monastics, this is a slow, contemplative praying of the Scriptures.

We can draw closer to God through the steps of reading the Word of God aloud, listening, contemplation, and prayer. We can do this on our own or with a group.

Father Luke Dysinger explains that Lectio Divina invites us to believe that our God is a loving Father. We can experience His love through His Word. We learn there is no secret place in us that can't be opened and offered to God. We discover what it means to be members of His royal priesthood.[4]

Our God longs for us. He has much to offer. He calls us. Let us answer, as the prophet Isaiah once did, "Here I am!"

Lucille's Story

Nowadays, it's not hard for Lucille to sit quietly. She lives on her own, and her home is tranquil. She invited me into her lovely home, and serenity flowed through my being as she welcomed me into her living room.

Her God and Lord is her constant Companion. She carries a calmness in her spirit that reaches out to others and soothes away the discord that can sit upon one's shoulders in a day. Her smile is gracious and kind.

You can tell that Lucille has been with Jesus, as the Scriptures say of His disciples (Acts 4:13).

"Distractions can be a problem," she admits. "Those can break a train of thought that God might be trying to get across. Then, there are ebbs and flows in the busyness of days." She looks around her cozy living room as she considers her words.

"It's harder when my routine gets knocked off. I plan the day, then I hear the Lord asking me which matters most to me—my schedule or the interruption He has brought to me."

It's a challenge for Lucille to rearrange her plans to accommodate the interruptions. If the Lord wants her to call someone, she usually discovers the call is timely. For her, it is all about people, after all, and not productivity—even productivity gained while doing the Lord's work. People come first.

"I desire that my actions and what my mouth says are the same."

Being silent before the Lord, listening for His voice has become natural for Lucille. It's something that she has come to. After a busy life, Lucille had to learn how to rest and be quiet before God. It took her a long while to discipline herself. She sought creativity as well as prayer to discover what she needed to change in order to make quietness doable.

What would it look like? What would need to go? What would she need to add? What would it take to help her minimize distractions and truly come into the presence of God?

Should she pray in a different room?

Should she be away from windows where some outside activity would attract her attention and then send her mind wandering?

Did the light glare too much? Would it mean a headache later?

How much did physical comfort matter? After all, her knees creaked.

Laughing, she said, "I put off praying on my knees for months because I was sure it would hurt. But I so wanted to be at the feet of Jesus. The day came when I determined to kneel. I grabbed pillows in preparation, but it surprised me that it didn't hurt at all. I thanked Jesus and asked Him to pull me back off my knees if it was going to interfere with our time together."

Lucille still kneels before Jesus. It's her latest spiritual practice. Communication seems to flow when she is on her knees. She has dedicated her "little bitty knees" to the Holy Spirit. "And then I do what He tells me to do."

Hearing from God is like a thought to Lucille. She makes sure it lines up with what Scripture says. She appreciates that it takes discipline to listen and recognize the thoughts that God brings to her.

"It's a way of growing more in relationship with Him. I am learning to discern His voice."

Lucille has had many voices coming into her mind and spirit over the years. From growing up in a large family, to raising her own, then different kinds of voices while working in occupations along the way. Sometimes it has been confusing to discriminate what they are saying or what she should do about them.

"I really appreciate what a kind Father God is to me. His character comes through as a Being of few words. He doesn't ramble. He is direct. Then He is silent. He has said what He meant to say, and now it's up to me to digest and process what He has said. Yes is yes, and no is no."

She knows she is to go and do whatever is needed.

A favorite passage of Scripture of Lucille's comes from the New Testament book of James. The writer exhorts us to count it all joy when we encounter various trials because these produce in us patience, completeness, wisdom, faith, and the humiliation to listen to the Holy Spirit teaching us (James 1:2–5).

Another passage of Scripture expresses that God's thoughts and ways are higher than ours (Isaiah 55:8–9).

"God is different from us. He is above us. He is 'other' than we are. He is THE Supreme Being. He has a right to expect anyone and everything to bow before Him. No matter what, even to the taking away of our loved ones."

He is trustworthy.

"It is well. It is well." Lucille sits back on her couch, a contented smile on her face.

"For I know the thoughts that I think toward you, says the Lord, thoughts of peace and not of evil, to give you a future and a hope" (Jeremiah 29:11).

Friendship Listening

I can't imagine the struggle Mrs. Job might have had with herself while learning to live with insight. It must have taken a great deal of thought before she could look under the surface of her husband's words to see his heart. As she listened to the debate between him and his friends, it must have required a great deal of self-restraint to keep silent.

Did she long for a female friend? Perhaps she needed someone to listen to her as she vented her fears and doubts. Maybe a friend could have asked clarifying questions, looking her in the eyes as she listened empathetically, much as Job's comforters had done before they opened their mouths. I can imagine Mrs. Job's snort of disgust at the thought of the men's foolish ramblings.

Perhaps the wisdom of another woman could have helped Mrs. Job discern the thoughts of her own soul—a kind woman who would sit in silence, listening with a soothing arm across her shoulders. Maybe it would be safe to spill the deep grief within and let healing happen. Oh, for such a friend!

It's written in Ecclesiastes that two are better than one. If one falls, the other can help her up again and provide the strength for leaning until the fallen one can walk on her own again (Ecclesiastes 4:9–10).

An old idiom also refers to two heads being better than one. Women tend to seek out companions to bounce their thoughts around. Many tangled threads have been straightened out in this way. Talking out a problem or an issue over tea or coffee can bring solutions. Regular outings with friends bring soul refreshment.

In the book of Job, God related to Job first. God knew that Job's heart was for Him, but Job needed testing to know that for himself. Before any other members of Job's household could manage their own lives before God, they needed a leader to be strong for them, to show them the way through adversity—to show God's sovereignty and His heart.

I believe that Mrs. Job drew strength from her husband's steadfast loyalty to God. She witnessed his weaknesses, but in her quiet listening to him, she sensed his unbreakable, underlying faith.

Mrs. Job did not have friends available to her at that time in her life, but God is always near. She wrestled with her emotions, but not until she called upon Him did she sense relief. Then, to her surprise, God did not talk to her about Job's arguments. Instead, He addressed her own concerns. Once again, He reassured her that He was present. God's friendship with us is a sure thing.

Mrs. Job discerned God's confidence in Job's faith, then His promise to her that she could trust Him. He would come through for her.

Building into the lives of others draws deeply from our own hearts. It takes listening to another level. The heart of God entwines with the hearts of broken people. Indeed, the very heart and body of Jesus was broken for our iniquities.

The word *iniquities* refer to immoralities, injustices, crimes, vices, and evils of every kind. Human beings have bents, or tendencies, toward all varieties of sin. Addictions abound and people wander, looking to depend on something or someone steady. Our children are trafficked as they get caught in the web of evil and unspeakable acts.

God calls us to minister to one another. He expects us to be available when we are called upon to attend to the despair of others.

In our listening, souls open and healing can begin.

Made in His image, God expects us to be His ears, His arms, His wisdom, and His love to one another.

Guyla's Story

In her own words, Guyla is "warped, wounded, and wacky." She grew up in a difficult family situation that left her "not okay," but she met Jesus early on. Recognizing Him as her Savior averted certain disaster.

"I don't see how anything positive or good can come without Him."

When Guyla was a twentysomething, God impressed on her that she would one day help people whom no one else could help. While she pondered that, a friend, a retired teacher, paid for Guyla to do studies in counseling. Her friend told her to pass it on, and now Guyla does.

Guyla worked at a church. Under Youth Pastor Joe's leadership, she ministered to troubled teens. All of them came from difficult home situations. All of them had encountered life-threatening circumstances at one time or another. Sometimes it was at home.

Because of Guyla's "warped, wounded, and wacky" past, God allowed her to make a major impact in the lives of several teens, then follow them into their adulthood. She called them her "kids," then her "twentysomethings," and now they are her "thirtysomethings."

"They gravitated to me because I have a 'yes face.'" She referred to the story of former United States President Teddy Roosevelt, who reportedly was once asked for a ride across a river because among the men running rafts, he was the one with the 'yes face.' Guyla has an infectious giggle that warms those around her. Kids wanted to laugh with her.

"I listened to them because I came from a secrecy and cover-up family. I did not want another generation to go through that."

Guyla wanted them to understand they had been heard when everyone else seemed to blow them off.

The Bible was studied, but often it was a time to just listen to angry girls. Studies that were available then were not generally geared toward healing brokenness. But before brains could work, lives had to be healed and protected.

"One thing I learned was to listen with one ear out and the other ear up." Guyla explains that with one ear she would listen to the girls; then, with the other ear, she would listen for wisdom from God. She relied on Holy Spirit discernment for godly wisdom, truth, and clarity in forms readily accepted and comprehended by broken teenagers.

Guyla let the kids come to her instead of trying to teach them. This way, she knew she was not giving them unwanted advice. When they did come to her for help, she said, "I gave them permission to throw me a raspberry if my advice to them was unpalatable. Sometimes they did, too, but they knew they could trust my love."

"They knew they could say anything to me, and I would not be horrified by it. I told them, 'I love you. There is nothing you could do or say that will change that. At some point, I will say or do something that will hurt or offend you. If I see it, I'll come to you and ask forgiveness. If I don't see it, please come to me, and I will ask forgiveness.'"

In this way, Guyla could show how God loves. She believes herself to be gracefully shockproof.

"I don't know if any of the kids had ever really been listened to before without judgment or other preconccived notions about them."

Guyla drew a parallel between Mrs. Job's outburst and the outcries of her broken teens. God's love is much bigger than our wails. He understands our human condition.

"In order to truly listen to them, I had to choose to mentally walk back into my life as I was growing up. Nobody was present for me." Guyla's own limits were stretched. The teens often told her she was not like others because of her willingness to not only walk with them through tragedies, but to go the extra mile to do it.

It was not easy to get behind social masks, but she was determined to reach them. Once, at a table setting, Guyla stooped under the table and audibly grumbled. Then she sat up with a wide, plastic smile on her face.

"Did you think that God doesn't see?" she asked.

They laughed at her, but the door opened then to sharing and healing.

Guyla giggles and says she considers herself "the poster child of what *not* to do." Her advice is, "Get help now. Don't wait for life to unravel first."

Guyla's students' twenties were "bumpy" rides. "It was like they were thrust into adulthood with broken training wheels." They are finding their way into their thirties. Some are juggling careers while married. Guyla loves seeing how God has worked the changes in their lives.

They still call her their spiritual mom. She loves that. They phone her for advice or to talk. Of course, these days texting is common. She still listens. Many of them consider her an extra grandma to their own children.

"We try to patch the fabric of the soul," Guyla mused, "but God comes along and says no. He then takes the soul back to where the tear occurred, and He weaves it back together."

Guyla's personal mission statement is: "Gracefully messy: to take every person I meet one step closer to Christ, and to create a place for life to happen."

And she does. The light of Christ giggles right through her.

"Trust in the Lord will all your heart, and lean not on your own understanding; in all your ways acknowledge Him, and He shall direct your paths" (Proverbs 3:5–6).

Practical Listening

All of us have had moments when we wish we'd listened to the voice inside that said, "STOP!"

One morning particularly, I should have listened to that inner voice.

I pulled into the mostly full parking lot, looking for an empty spot. Ah—several parking spots were empty facing the street. My inclination (read that as "still, small voice") was to pull into one of those spaces. They looked safe. But another car left an opening closer to the door of the building where my meeting was scheduled. I pulled into a gap behind a truck and confidently sauntered into the building to gather with my buddies.

After my appointment, I rounded my car from the rear and drove to another destination to do an errand that caused me to open the trunk. It wasn't until I got home that I saw the front. Sigh. The dents were in the middle, and the license plate was folded up like an accordion. When did I do that? Wouldn't I have noticed?

As strange as this sounds, I did not see the note that had been folded into a corner of the windshield until I got home. The information on it made it evident that the fellow who backed into my car felt terrible. When I called him, I could tell he was angry at himself, though he was very polite. I would have been figuratively knocking my head against the wall had I been in his place. I forgave him. After getting his insurance information—gladly given, I might add—I took the car to the mechanics. Those good guys fixed it all. The whole episode is forgiven and sort of forgotten.

If I had only listened to that nudge before I parked my car, all the fuss would have been avoided—for the driver of the truck as well as for myself.

Perhaps if I had spent more time that morning in prayer, listening for God's voice to speak to me, I would have paid attention in the parking lot.

Listening for God's voice doesn't necessarily require a theological treatise. God speaks to us in many ways: through the physical world around us, music, people, projects, or an impression—we *just know.*

We're familiar with most practical listening. We take notes when we hear lectures or sermons, or we may be in Bible studies where we are required to take notes.

Another way to listen practically is to journal our thoughts. It's a good idea to write down our thoughts, along with what we learn, because then we can see what's whirling around in our heads. The words make sense as they appear before our eyes. We can identify what is going on in our souls as we write it down; therefore, we can acknowledge our emotions. It's a way of listening to ourselves, and sometimes it is a way of discerning God's intent for us as well.

We write down our thoughts and listen in several practical ways.

We read the Bible and write down what God impresses on us. Nothing in life will work if we don't start by seeking God first.

We pour out our anguish before God. Only He sees this and has the wisdom to keep us from offending others with misspoken words or actions.

We remember what the Lord has done in the past and are encouraged to move forward.

We pass down to the next generation the lessons we have learned so they can see how God was faithful.

We organize our thoughts and actions. In this way of listening, we understand how God leads and guides us.

We pray through God's Word as well as our own words. In recording prayers, situations, and answers, we see how God loves us. Our spirits then listen for His words of life, and we won't lose them if we have written them.

Listening, no matter how we do it, is about everyday living. Our Father God is as involved with our days as we are. He goes with us, even when we ignore His impressions on our souls in order to go our own way.

Gerry's Story

Gerry worked at a grade school. After fourteen years of working in the copy/management room, she began assisting the secretary, Carrie, with various office duties. But Gerry had other duties that took her out of the office. She enjoyed working with the children on lunchroom duty and at recess, and working with teachers in several different classrooms helping students.

It became apparent that Carrie was overwhelmed with the projects it took to keep a school running. Soon a new administrative assistant position opened, and she urged Gerry to apply. They had built a friendship and had fun working together.

"Gerry, you need to apply for this job. We work well together. I want you to apply."

It seemed like a good fit, though Gerry felt uncomfortable with the idea. She ignored a niggle of doubt at the back of her mind. Since childhood, she'd nurtured a desire to work as a secretary. Because she liked Carrie, Gerry applied for the job. She went through the interview process. Her peers made up the panel. It seemed to go well, but Gerry did not get the job.

The rejection hurt. Gerry saw these people every day. They knew what she could do, yet they hired another woman to fill the position. How did this reflect on how they saw her? Would this affect anything she did afterward? After a year, the new employee decided to leave, and the position was open again.

"Gerry, apply again. I'd really like you to be in the front office to work with me," Carrie pleaded.

This time, Gerry heard the Lord speak in her heart: "You shouldn't be doing this. It isn't where I want you." Gerry wouldn't be with the children she loved to help. But the position was open for a second time, after all. Surely, she should try.

"I knew in my heart that I shouldn't do it, but I didn't want to let Carrie down."

Once more, she went through the interview process. This time Gerry sensed a door slam shut. Another woman was hired, someone not previously employed in their building. Gerry knew nearly everybody working there, but not this woman. The panel had chosen someone from the outside instead of Gerry—someone with computer knowledge that Gerry lacked, someone with secretarial experience. But couldn't they have trained Gerry? She could learn.

Devastated, Gerry had to gather her courage to keep going. Concentrating on spit-spot cleaning of her desk, she contemplated how to welcome the new employee. She decided she would put flowers on the desk and make a welcome sign. It was hard, but it was the right thing to do.

As she labored through disgruntlement, Gerry received notes from teachers with words of encouragement and love.

"A couple of people on the interview team told me they had fought for me to have the new position. It brought me joy to know they cared that much. The Lord was using so many people to encourage me that it felt like a loving hug from Him. When one door shuts, the Lord opens another. He had another position in mind for me, but not the one I was trying to do to please my friend."

Soon, a job in the LAP (Learning Assistance Program) opened up, one that would mean helping individual children hone their reading skills.

"I didn't even have to apply for that one; I was asked by the LAP teacher to take it. The Lord had that already in place, knowing I loved being with children, not just adults. God knew where He wanted me to be. He knew, too, I would be much happier working with children."

Gerry's classroom was in a small closet-like room, but she put chairs and a table there to welcome struggling students who needed extra help with their reading skills. The opportunity to be with the children in the lunchroom, at recess, and in classrooms was still part of her job. Gerry would thrive here. She knew the hand of God had provided.

"I was a lay teacher. This job was less stressful. Everything turned out for the best. In this experience, I learned it's best to listen to the Lord's promptings in the first place, instead of someone else. He has a way of working things out for our best interests and abilities."

"For I know what I have planned for you," says the Lord. "I have plans to prosper you, not to harm you. I have plans to give you a future filled with hope" (Jeremiah 29:11 NET).

Listening While on the Path

What sweet companionship God must have had with Adam and Eve before sin ruined it. How intently the first human beings must have listened to the words God spoke in those days.

I have often wished I could have been there to walk with Him. Would we hold hands as we strolled through His garden? Would we talk about the day's events, or would we swing our hands in silent closeness?

I love looking at God's marvelous creation in real life. I also love taking photos to look at later. As I shuffle through them, I see a picture of a path through the trees. Out of sight, where it looks like the path takes a turn to the right, the sun's rays diffuse into a yellow-white screen behind which the trees can be faintly seen. Further on ahead, the path continues.

Sometimes I relive moments or imagine scenes that could happen in these settings. I stare at this picture and hear words of Jesus swirl in my head. He is speaking to His disciples about leaving them and what lay ahead. He said He had many things to tell them, but they could not bear them then (John 16:12).

It's still true. He has many things to speak to us, but we can't bear them. How many times I have yearned to know answers to things I could not understand! When they come, I am glad I didn't have those answers when I first asked. He has many things to speak to our hearts, but we often don't know how to listen. We don't know what to do with His words.

Looking deeper into the picture, I notice that the path does not veer to the right where the sun's rays are, but it goes straight ahead. What a surprise! I gaze intently before I can see the truth. The road goes straight. The sun comes alongside. The picture invites me in. The impression of His words floats deep into my soul:

> You see, Child, I still walk close to you. Last week, I begged you to come away with Me. You see that I have straightened the path and lit the way. I've given a glorious way. Listen to My words of love. You know that no one comes to My Father except through Me. How eagerly I long to bring you, My bride, to My Father! He already approves. Come, let's walk together.

Child of God, He longs for you and me to walk intimately with Him. He's prepared the road. He is the light by our side. He longs to speak words of love to us. He wants to take us to His Father. Can we hear Him? Can we believe in His love? Are we ready to bear His words?

Let us allow Him to take our hands, and let us go where He leads. Let us listen to His loving plans for our lives.

"I still have many things to say to you, but you cannot bear them now" (John 16:12).

Meditation Questions

1. How can you be satisfied with leaving the whys in the hands of God?

2. Have you found wisdom in learning to listen? If so, has your life been enriched?

3. Have you experienced a time of deep listening? What was it like?

4. When did you come alongside someone else in their time of need?

5. Can you remember times when you have ignored God's voice within you and done the opposite of that nudge? What was the result?

6. How do you listen to God?

Journal Question

What is your "cool of the day" moment when you meet with God? Write down what it means to you to know that Jesus waits to take your hand and stroll among the trees to whisper secrets to you. What might that be like?

Prayer

"Let the words of my mouth and the meditation of my heart be acceptable in Your sight, O Lord, my strength and my Redeemer" (Psalm 19:14).

Abba Daddy, thank You for hearing our words as we pour them out before You. You are so kind, gentle, and loving in Your dealings with us. Yet we are dull to heed Your voice in our hearts. Forgive us for not listening to *Your* heart. Thank You for waiting for us in the beauty of the cool of the day. Your companionship is as sparkling and pure to us as a refreshing breeze. Come and fill us with Your sweet, sweet Spirit.

SIX

Believe and Trust

And the Lord restored Job's losses when he prayed for his
friends. Indeed the Lord gave Job twice as much
as he had before.
Job 42:10

It could have happened this way . . .

Mrs. Job sighed as she glanced around the room. Palm trees
stood at every entrance. Rugs covered the floors and tap-
estries decorated the walls. Food-and-drink-filled tables lined the
perimeter of the room, all provided by the bridegroom.

Her own elegant linen gown fell in graceful folds across her
chest, draped down from the jeweled fastenings at her shoulder.

Job's and her own eldest daughter, Jemimah, would wed Shugi
today. Shugi's father had invited all the community, as well as family, to join in this happy celebration.

To think that she sat among two other daughters and seven
sons while witnessing this grand occasion! There had been a time
when she was sure life held nothing but loss and horror. Those

dreadful years lived in her heart along with the losses of her first ten children, but unexpectedly, the one true God had restored her husband's life. Her own life had blossomed as Job grew stronger.

She remembered when Job had disappeared into the desert one day. She thought she'd never see him again. She'd sobbed every day in panic. What would happen to her? Without her husband or children, she would be alone. How would she survive? A week or so later, he had suddenly returned. His boils were gone, and his face shone like the sun.

"What happened, Husband? You are well?"

He bowed low, and she had to lean forward to hear him. "God has spoken."

She didn't know what to think.

The next day, Eliphaz, Bildad, and Zophar came to her husband. They bowed low as they sought his forgiveness for having accused him before God. It seemed the Most High had shown them how wrong they were and directed them to ask Job to forgive them. He did—readily.

After that, things happened so fast it sent Mrs. Job's head spinning. Her husband once again put his business acumen to work to build commerce, amass herds, and hire servants. He moved the two of them back up the hill and out of the dung.

But Mrs. Job never forgot those dreadful days. She made sure she shared food and other usable items wherever she saw need. No one would go hungry or be cold at night if she could help it.

God had restored a family to them too. Her shame was over! Their daughters were distinguished for their beauty throughout the land, and their father settled an inheritance upon each of them, as he had done for all seven sons.

Jemimah sat in the middle of the room. Her golden gown swirled around her. The crown of jewels, woven through the tresses of her dark hair, sparkled through the curls piled upon her head.

Golden earrings swung gently by her bronze cheeks. Her brown eyes were softened by the smile on her lips.

"My daughter," Job's deep voice rumbled, "according to the marriage covenant, your inheritance is yours to use as you wish. May it grow, blessing you and your posterity. I love you, my dear." He kissed her cheek and came to sit beside his wife.

He clasped her hand on his lap, smiling tenderly into her eyes. "Our God is good, is He not, Wife?"

"Husband, He is always good." She leaned her shoulder against him.

The handsome young groom bent over his bride and pulled a gossamer veil over her, declaring, "She is my wife." He reached for the perfume and sprinkled it over Jemimah's head. Then he knelt before her and lifted her hand, gently slipping a ring on her finger and pressing a kiss on it.

Mrs. Job sighed happily. There had been a time when she thought she would never see a daughter married. *Thank You, Most High, for all honor and glory and blessing belong to You.*

Meanwhile, in the book of Job . . .

Job, with his wife by his side, suffered through a very painful season of their lives without knowing why. They endured the loss of everything but each other, including ten children. Their circumstances changed as a result. Job even lost his health. His friends were no help to him, and he continued to ask God for an audience.

He received that audience, but it wasn't what he expected. He thought he would demand answers and God would give them. Instead, Job found himself in a whirlwind, with God throwing questions at him from all sides—questions Job could not begin to answer because he was not God.

Throughout all of this, Job remained faithful. And God rewarded him.

When God Restores

God restored to Job twice as much as he had lost. We are told that Job's brothers and sisters returned to his fellowship. His acquaintances from before also returned. It seems they all brought gifts to him. I do wonder where they were when he and his wife needed them, since this is the first mention of any of them.

Job's lands, livestock, and wealth were all greater than he had before.

Along with seven sons, Job and his wife had three more daughters. At the end of Job's story, God named Job's daughters. It is written that they were the most beautiful women in the land. Job granted to them the same inheritance given to his sons. These were not dowries that would pass into the hands of an eventual husband. The girls would have the same control over their own inheritances that the boys did.

Perhaps the reward of a second set of ten children was worth a season of suffering. The first ten children would not be forgotten, but God added ten more to Job's quiver. This would be wealth indeed.

The fame of Job's daughters for their beauty suggests that grace made a way for Mrs. Job. It's a legendary axiom that outward beauty reflects what is within. Where would these most magnificent women have learned such splendor if not guided by the hand of a loving and beautiful mother? Possibly, the daughters could be the reward for obedience and faithfulness on the part of their mother.

What stands out in this story is that Job's wife is not mentioned after her initial outburst. Since Job's restoration is listed specifically, I believe that if God had replaced Mrs. Job, He would have stated it. I like to think she repented and learned to follow her husband's lead in bowing before the one true God.

Forgiveness is at the core of God's heart. If there had been no forgiveness for Mrs. Job, then what would we learn by her initial outburst? How could we know that grace would cover our own outbursts when we are disappointed? Could there be second chances?

He restores our souls, Psalm 23 assures us. God is merciful, and He gives us refreshment. He does not replace us when we mess up, either. He is *for* us! He gives us every opportunity to come back to Him and move forward according to His plan for us.

Although restoration happened within Job's lifetime, it's not always a personal experience. Sometimes it can be a family outcome far down the road.

We are an impatient generation. We expect instant results, but God sees long term. He sees how the consequences of our actions will affect generations to come for centuries after us.

Decisions we make don't just affect us. Our children and grandchildren may reap what we sow, or they may benefit by the good we have done. History and even governments hang on decisions of individuals.

Our thoughts and actions matter.

The cross of Jesus provides us complete forgiveness and healing. His resurrection restores us to complete fellowship with God for all eternity, even when the circumstances we see don't resemble love or mercy at all.

When God restores, He does it all the way!

"And the Lord restored Job's losses when he prayed for his friends. Indeed the Lord gave Job twice as much as he had before" (Job 42:10).

Cathy's Story

World War II raged on.

Jun, a Japanese widow with six children, resided in a barrack with five other families. Herded secretly from their homes, these families were transported to an American detention compound called Minidoka, in Jerome, Idaho, where they were incarcerated for the duration of the war. Properties were confiscated; sometimes families were separated. Jun lost her farm.

Divided into units with sheets and blankets hung between them, the families in Barrack 36 became their own neighborhood. They shared one potbellied stove in their building.

Several barracks made up a small city within barbed-wire perimeters. Organization fell into these positions: block managers, block representatives, and co-op delegates.

They learned to do laundry together, grow a garden in the middle of the dusty terrain, and can to preserve their produce. They raised livestock. A camp hospital served their medical needs. Children were educated at an education center. Sports were organized for young people. A postal service served them in the camp. A Parent-Soldier Association was formed to help parents support their sons who were fighting the war in the US armed forces.

Barracks inmates refined a philosophy together: *Shikata ga nai, Shoganai* (it cannot be helped) and *Kodomo no tame ni* (for the sake of the children). They made their lives as normal as possible under terrible circumstances.

When the war ended, Jun's children spread out throughout the US. She would go to each family for a prolonged stay before moving to the next offspring's family. Jun, Cathy's paternal grandmother, would share young Cathy's room whenever she visited. That was okay with Cathy, and those memories comfort her even now.

Since Cathy had grown up after World War II, she knew very little about how her family spent the war. She'd heard whispers, but didn't understand. As a child, she remembers her Grandma Jun as "quiet, nurturing, and she talked funny. But she never scolded."

When Grandma Jun came to visit, she was patient with Cathy's many queries about her family. She would give the answers to the whispers Cathy had heard. Because her father passed away when she was nine years old, Cathy's memory of him is dim. She could not ask her mother questions. "They just didn't talk about things."

"Looking back, I realize Grandma was joyful no matter what life had to offer her. I've tried to imagine walking out what she'd had to do. What would it look like? Yet she was always cheerful."

Cathy explained the Japanese generations in America in segments.

Issei ("ee-say"): the first immigration generation from Japan to the United States.

Nisei ("nee-say"): the second generation, made up of US-born citizens of Japanese ethnicity.

Sansei ("sen-say"): the third generation, comprised of US citizens born of Nisei parents.

In 2019, Cathy had an opportunity to make a trip to Jerome, Idaho, as part of the Minidoka Pilgrimage, to the former concentration camp at Minidoka with other Japanese internment descendants.

"When I heard about this, it became real, and I wanted to go. I walked the flat, windy expanse in sandy sage. The wind really howls, and it's eerie. One barrack is left to tour. I saw the dining hall. It hit me that this really happened!"

Some camp survivors are vocal, participating in protests at Fort Sill, Oklahoma, but most of those Cathy met are joyful they survived. She attributes that to the parents' determination to make the best of their situation at the time for the sake of the children.

Because of the pilgrimage, Sansei generations have a shared experience with their families. Going on this pilgrimage gave Cathy a sense of history.

"Without the pictures of what the camp looked like then, you would never know it had been there. How quickly the memory goes away!"

"I honed in on my grandmother. Her experience came alive for me. How she went through that terrifying time on her own, with six children to care for, amazed me. Her abiding legacy to me is a quiet, peaceful one."

In June 2019, Dr. Satsuki Ina spoke to Japanese generations visiting at Fort Sill, Oklahoma. With the lonely barrack in sight, dust blowing, his talk vibrated like a song. He detailed living through the pain in the detention camps and expressed the determination to never forget. He ended his speech with these words:

> We will not forget you.
> We will not be silent.
> We will come back for you.
> And we will bring others
> Until you are free.

Trust God

At times, God gives us opportunities to do things we don't believe we can do. He stretches us. He waits for us to reach for Him. He longs for our growth.

When we set out to train our eyes to see beyond our current circumstances and trust God for results, our growth begins. When answers don't immediately come, we determine to be confident that our God will see to our ultimate good. We walk more deeply with God at the end of our testing than we did at the beginning.

Music stirs us at the heart level. God uses it to reach us in a unique way. I recently heard a sweet song about hand and heart in the language of love.[1]

The lyric of the song says if the hero had all of eternity, it would not be enough to tell his sweetheart how much he loves her. God has shown us His love from all eternity past and will continue to show us forever.

Whose hand has more meaning than the hand of Father God? When I meditate upon this, I picture His hand sitting on the top of my head and turning it in the direction He wants me to go, much like the hand of a child's father when steering him through a crowd. God holds our circumstances, our lives, and our loved ones in His hands. No matter how it looks, we can trust His hand.

As a child, I learned about the Sacred Heart of Jesus. Usually depicted as a heart burning in flames, it reminds me of the burning bush that Moses saw. The idea is that God's heart burns for us continually and passionately. He longs to spend time with us. He longs for us to bring our cares to Him. He has plans for our good. He tells us again and again in His Word. He reaches for us—every day.

God ardently loves us. Jesus showed us His love by giving Himself in our place in a death meant to swallow us. We are helpless to avoid falling into the pit for eternity, but Jesus put Himself in the place of sacrifice, and we fall into Him instead of the pit. When He raised Himself out of the abyss, He went home to heaven to prepare a place for us. He waits there for the right time to return for His people so we can live with Him for eternity. His love is His promise.

What about us? If we are incapable of showing God our love for Him, we can give Him the one thing He asks—ourselves. In the light of His love for us, how can this gift of our lives be a sacrifice?

We walk the path He sets before us. Our eyes gaze at the distant horizon. We place ourselves in a period of silence to listen. In the tranquility and the silence of our souls, He speaks to us. We surrender all those hidden things to His care. Because His hand is upon us. Because His heart is for us. Because His love is set upon us.

We might catch a glimpse of the eternity Jesus said He has gone to prepare for us.

Our God is trustworthy.

"He has made everything beautiful in its time. Also He has put eternity in their hearts, except that no one can find out the work that God does from beginning to end" (Ecclesiastes 3:11).

Confidence in God

I played on my high school tennis team. I can still feel the satisfying SMACK when the ball hits the sweet spot in the racket on a return volley. I remember the adrenaline pumping as I rushed the net with overhead smashes that skimmed across my opponent's court at lightning speed.

I'll always remember one match I played. My opponent was bigger than me—both taller and larger. As a result, she had more power. She also played games within a game. She used tricks, as if she'd twisted a knee or ankle, or hurt her back or arm. I'm sure this was done to throw me off my game. It worked. I felt sorry for her. Big mistake!

It wasn't until I reached my coach that I learned the whole team match had depended on the outcome of my individual match. The team lost that day. I wilted. But my coach affirmed that I'd played well. She went on to say I'd had to contend with actions that had no business on a tennis court. I have an idea she lodged a complaint wherever coaches do that. I could have called a time-out and consulted with my coach. I wish I had done so.

I learned to look to my coach, especially during a contest.

I also learned a bit about discernment. What is real, trickery, or false? Things may look one way to me, but observers may see what's really going on.

I learned to conduct myself with decorum, even if my opponent plays foul. If provoked, I can act with dignity. It's a decision I must make in my head before a situation presents the opportunity.

Our Enemy uses tricks and feigns weakness before slamming a win over us. We may feel like an underdog. We may feel discouraged. We may feel like a loser. But our Coach is always on our side. He's ready to pat us on the back and give us tips and encouragement at any point to improve our game.

If it appears we have lost—game, set, match—it falls behind us when He tells us that we played well, no matter the obstacles!

Keeping our eyes on our Coach, as well as the ball, gives us the confidence to go WIN!

There is a great purpose to our lives. When battles commence, the banner of our God flies over us. We can be confident in this: Jesus is for us! He has already won the victory at the cross and the empty tomb. The battles we experience are the skirmishes that are reminiscent of the last kicks before defeat. It's our privilege to show the grace and magnificence of our God to those who don't yet know the battle is won.

Always, we can be confident in the character of our God.

We don't have to understand it when things don't look right or when we lose. We can trust Him because He knows the end from the beginning. He is good. All the time. No matter what. Even if we don't get it.

Reinforcing this, I again read from the writings of Oswald Chambers. Chambers said that though we may ask God what our future will be, He may not tell us. He is more interested in revealing to us who He is. It is our job to believe in a miracle-working God and move out in surrender to Him.[2]

When I read that God seeks to reveal His character rather than His intentions, it was a new idea to me. When I looked for answers, I never imagined that God Himself *is* the Answer. Learning to trust Him in new ways challenged me. If my circumstances don't change in the way I have prayed, I can still have the conviction that God is good and that nothing is too hard for Him to handle. I can move forward boldly.

We are safe in His hands. Our Savior promises to be with us—all the time, no matter what. This is our comfort, our certainty, and our courage. Only in the hands of God are we able to move forward to our destiny with assurance.

"For whatever is born of God overcomes the world. And this is the victory that has overcome the world—our faith" (1 John 5:4).

The love of our God and Father continues to flow. Every perfect gift comes from Him. We can be confident in Him.

His presence is continually with us.

He watches over us constantly.

He understands our hopes and dreams.

He hears us no matter how faint our words.

He guides us in any circumstance.

He answers all our requests.

He is our loving Father, encouraging us.

He persistently does what is best for us.

He offers us faith daily.

His promises are alive.

His grace is always extended.

His forgiveness is forever.

He offers His kingdom to us.

He has raised us from the dead.

He promises to return for us.

Let us joyfully and gratefully praise Him!

Celebrate

What is a celebration? A time of great festivity, a party, a gala. A time when people gather to share merriment or, more soberly, a commemoration. It's when a crowd gets together to do something special.

We celebrate birthdays, graduations, reunions, and anniversaries of all kinds. We honor our loved ones by celebrating milestones in their lives.

In the Old Testament, we learn that King David danced as the ark of God was brought home to Jerusalem. "Then David danced before the Lord with all his might" (2 Samuel 6:14). The ark arrived "with shouting and with the sound of the trumpet" (2 Samuel 6:15). A great celebration with dancing, playing of instruments, and feasting happened that day. It was probably a national day of celebration. How exciting it must have been, with dancing in the streets!

Weddings provide such occasions for jubilance. Months of planning drill down to make sure the tiniest details are just right. Anticipation builds as the date gets closer. The perfect bridal gown is absolutely vital, the cake must be flawless, the flowers fresh, and the bridesmaid dresses and groomsman cummerbunds must match. Harmony is of the utmost importance.

For a long period of time, the occasion is in the future. A few ideas are tossed around and lists are made. Plans begin to be set into motion. As the event date gets closer, the activity level rises. The location is selected. Then, before you know it, it's the week of the affair. Suddenly, you are decorating. The splendid rental cutlery and linens arrive, place settings are set out, and the centerpieces are gorgeous.

You can't wait for your guests to arrive.

It must have been this way for the Job family. The time of deep, terrible darkness was past. Job spent what must have seemed like a second lifetime building up a home and business once again. God restored to him twice what was lost. Perhaps he carried his first ten children in his heart, but that did not stop the celebration with the second ten children. It may be that his happiness was all the sweeter because his wife had come through the painful journey with him and shared his rewards.

Gratitude to God for bringing them out of the darkness would be the best reason to celebrate. What festivity could be better than the wedding of Job's eldest daughter? Job also had an inheritance to bestow upon her. As a father, that must have given him great satisfaction.

I can imagine Job and Mrs. Job standing together, arms around each other, as they greeted guests and watched their children dance. Overcoming darkness brought them a deeper faith. That is something to celebrate!

Weddings are close to the heart of God. His original design meant that two should become one. He made us to reflect His image. One day, as history closes, a marriage feast will be prepared in heaven. I believe Jesus waits for that day with great eagerness. The church, which together makes up His bride, will be assembled at His table. We, His bride, will be fully united with Jesus, our Groom.

Soon He will come!

Start dancing! It's time!

As Mrs. Job said, "Thank You, Most High, for all honor and glory and blessing belong to You."

Debbie's Story

Debbie found the man God meant for her. It had been a long wait, and she'd wondered if it would ever happen.

Debbie's family comes from the Philippines. Her father came home one day with an immigrant visa to the United States and moved his surprised family—Debbie, her mother, and two younger sisters—across an ocean. Debbie was twelve. The cultural switch was a challenge for her.

Much to the amazement of her peers, Debbie didn't date during her high school years.

"The Filipino culture has very definite 'idealized timelines,'" Debbie explains. "In the Filipino culture, you court the person you are going to marry. It's intentional. A girl goes to school, she gets a job, she courts with her man, they marry and have children."

Only it didn't work that way for Debbie.

After she graduated high school, she went back to the Philippines. It had been six years since she'd left. She met again her child-hood crush. As Filipino culture dictated, they courted, and family were always around to chaperone. Debbie expected to marry him. She stayed a month before returning to the US. They exchanged letters for three years (before email became the mode of communi-cation). She thought they were getting to know one another fairly well.

However, distance, college, and religious differences ended the relationship. Devastated, Debbie took her broken heart to her youth leader for counsel. "It felt strange to be sharing my love life, but he prayed for me."

As the saying goes, when one door closes, another opens. Deb-bie is musical. She sings and plays piano and keyboard. When she auditioned, she was asked to join a band called Free Spirit, through the Free Methodist Church. She made a commitment of a year, as requested, to play at churches, youth camps, and conferences.

"Looking back," Debbie muses, "God ordained this. I never could have done it if I had continued in that relationship." She learned to trust God for her future. As an introvert, this experience forced her to grow while performing. She sang solos and played instruments as well.

Once the year ended, Debbie looked around for her next ad-venture. With nine hundred dollars in her bank account and no job, she relocated to another US city. "I trusted God. I really had no fear." She found two jobs and worked them both at the same time. One was short-term, but the other supported her for seven years.

"It was a God thing. He opened doors and supplied all my needs according to His riches in glory!"

By now, the "idealized timeline" had been disrupted in Deb-bie's life. She dated the American way, but again endured a broken heart when a romance ended. Finally, she asked herself what was keeping her in that city, so she decided to return home to the Pacific Northwest to be with her family, bringing her back into the local Filipino culture in her hometown. During community gatherings, the big question always addressed to her was, "Why aren't you married yet?" She could only shrug her shoulders. Where *was* he?

One more time, an opportunity came about for Debbie to visit the Philippines. She packed up and flew across the Pacific Ocean. She met a nice man who seemed to share her interests in music and ministry. She thought again, "This is it!" Alas, another broken heart. She came home to the US and took time off from all ministry to heal.

"I was empty this time. I had no joy to share. No singing. Just nothing."

Oftentimes, it's interesting that what we seek has been near us all the time. Arnold's family and Debbie's family had been friends for years. Both Debbie and Arnold were healing from hurts. Both were searching for what God would have for them. Debbie's mom ran into Arnold one day and invited him home for lunch. When her mom encouraged her to call Arnold after lunch that day, Debbie hesitated. She wasn't ready to dive into anything, but Mom said, "Just be his friend."

Debbie called him. A new friendship developed. Arnold confessed he'd always liked her, but Debbie was hesitant. At the counsel of her church's worship director, she asked Arnold to put a pause on their times together for one month. The last week of that month, Arnold left town to check out a job in another state. At first, Debbie felt carefree, but by the sixth day of Arnold's trip, she started missing him. Finally, she realized God was tugging her heart in Arnold's direction. When he came home, they began courting—yes, the Filipino way.

When the wedding day arrived, family gathered, along with many friends from the Filipino community. Friends from Debbie's and her parents' churches attended. Much to Debbie's delight, her girlfriend from her old band flew, with her new husband, from Pennsylvania to Washington State to attend.

The wedding incorporated traditional elements of a typical Filipino wedding, as well as Christian elements like partaking of communion. At the reception, the Silangan Dancers of the Filipino-American Association of the Inland Empire shared three dances and showcased the culture to American guests. The party lasted six hours, from the beginning of the ceremony to the end of the reception. They ate, danced, laughed, and celebrated the wedding day without a single glitch!

"This was such a blessing, because so many told me that something almost always goes wrong," Debbie observed. "When something is planned by man, it doesn't always go smoothly, but when it's planned by God, it's an unforgettable celebration!"

"God has many surprises, and He changes your heart to what is best for you," Debbie said. She lists the things God has taught her:

- His presence is constant.
- He doesn't always take away pain, but He carries her through it.
- God's plans are always good, even when they are different from hers.
- His timing is always right, even when the wait is excruciating.
- He never lets go. He always comes after her wherever she wanders.
- Brokenness brought her to the place of relinquishing her control to God's control.
- God always provides. He has shown it time and again, even when the not knowing is hard.
- Worship is much sweeter. She once worshipped through pain. Now she worships in celebration.

Joy

One winter morning God gave me a beautiful gift as I looked out the window. Two whitetail deer were curled up in my backyard on the frost-tipped grass. It seemed to me that they should be shivering with cold, but they looked perfectly comfortable. Occasionally, they lifted their heads to sniff the air and twitch their ears.

As cars whizzed by on the nearby road, the does were peaceful, purely "being" as they were created. I wondered if God savored a moment of joy as He watched those graceful creatures that morning.

I carried this picture of joy with me during the next week. I rested in it over and over.

With this image in mind, I pondered the meaning of joy. Much deeper than happiness, joy abides with us through the dark times of life.

- Joy gives us courage to keep going.
- Joy assures us that God is with us.
- Joy allows God to take our spiritual hands in His.
- Joy frees us to go where He leads.
- Joy undergirds the sorrows of our lives.

Greg Ogden, in his book *Discipleship Essentials*, said, "Joy is living under the pleasure of the Father's delight in you."[3] Think of that. Father God delights in us. Joy bursts upon us! Ogden continues: "Joy transcends circumstances."[4]

It's a curious thing that joy can coexist with sorrow, yet it transcends the sorrow by its very nature. Think of the loss of a grandfather and the birth of a new baby in the same family on the same day. It's a mystery how joy and grief occur side by side. The joy overrides the sorrow.

Ogden says, "Joy can coexist with suffering and grief. Joy is stable, because it is rooted in hope."[5]

Joy is rooted in hope. Scripture tells us hope does not disappoint because God's love is poured into us by His Holy Spirit, who is always with us. This is a wonderful promise to carry. What a great reason to be joyful.

Mother Teresa of Calcutta wrote in *My Life for the Poor*:

> Joy is prayer. Joy is strength. Joy is love. Joy is a net of love by which you can catch souls. God loves a cheerful giver. One gives most who gives with joy. The best way to show our gratitude to God and people is to accept everything with joy. A joyful heart is the normal result of a heart burning with love. Never let anything so fill you with sorrow as to make you forget the joy of Christ risen. This I tell my sisters. This I tell to you.[6]

Underlying all things in our lives is the love of God. The fullness of joy is knowing that Jesus is with us. The very stream of life is the joy flowing from Him to us. His grace keeps calling us close to Him.

Joy, the confidence that He will always carry us, anchors us. God will be glorified in us.

Jeanne's Story

"I am an optimist," Jeanne will readily admit. "All my life, songs have played in my head. I can't help but sing along. I can finish songs other people quote." Anyone who knows her can vouch for the joy she exudes.

Her high school yearbook team secretly chose Scriptures to put under graduates' pictures in the annual. When the books were revealed, Jeanne saw written under her photo, "A merry heart does good like a medicine" (Proverbs 17:22).

Life hasn't always been like a song for her, though. Jeanne's father passed away when she was nine. Her mom had no job, could not drive, and had three children to support.

Jeanne recalls her mom gazing out the window, crying. "There will be no more pheasant dinners," she sighed. Jeanne's dad used to hunt to provide food for the family.

"Right then, a pheasant hit the window and dropped dead. Later, Mom said, 'I knew if God cared enough to send me a pheasant dinner, He would take care of us, and I could trust Him.'"

That was the first time Jeanne realized God wasn't some nebulous Being somewhere, but a Father who really cared about His children.

She went to college to become a nurse, where she met and married her husband, Jim, and they started their family. Soon after, Jim's mother experienced a heart attack, which necessitated a move across the country to help her. For a while, they assisted Jim's parents with health issues and with caring for his younger brother, still in school.

Jim found a new job. However, it turned out to be in a different town. That left Jeanne at home alone with two small children, Jennifer and Bethany, and pregnant with another child. Three months went by before Jim was able to get home. By then, baby Mike was on his way to birth.

"My water broke. I called Jim and then some friends. One friend picked me up to go to the hospital, and another one stayed with Jennifer and Bethany. I didn't know Jim had had an accident on his job, but he drove to us anyway. Mike had been born by the time Jim found us all at the hospital."

The family moved again, this time to Kennewick, Washington, a city in a desert. Bethany suffered with asthma. When they experienced their first dust storm the night they moved in, Bethany had to be hospitalized with pneumonia. With a new baby and a child in the hospital, coping was hard for Jeanne. When her sister, Carolyn, came to help, Jim drove all the way to the Spokane airport to get her.

"She thought she was coming to meet baby Mike, but she helped me so much. She came at the right time. The amazing thing is that she bought her ticket three months before Mike was born. It showed me God really sees my struggles and cares. Only He would know how much I would need her at just that time."

After a few years, Jim experienced heart trouble and underwent open-heart surgery. This was tough on the young family. Jeanne's nursing skills came into play as she juggled Jim's care and new health instructions with the needs of her growing children. Somehow, Jeanne had assurance they would be all right. In all this time, melodies always played in her mind.

As Mike grew, he hit his teens in rebellion. As he slid further and further into trouble, his parents could not help him. The more they tried, the further out of reach he went. At the same time, Bethany felt neglected when her parents' attention kept being claimed by her brother.

Jeanne felt the pressure. "There wasn't enough of me to go around." She struggled through the deep testing of her soul. As any parent with a wayward child knows, the pain is too deep for words. Jeanne would try to pray.

"I couldn't form words. I could only groan before God."

Finally, she heard in her heart, "Mike is not yours. He's Mine. I have a plan for his life."

"I knew then how much God really loved me. If I loved my son that much, no matter what he had done, then I could better understand that God loved me even more."

The day came when Mike turned a corner, which was cause for rejoicing, yet troubles were not over. A car accident left Jeanne with serious health issues that she has lived with since then. She still heard the music in her soul.

When Jim died, Jeanne had the assurance she would see him

again one day when it would be her turn to make that journey. Her children were great supports to her.

"I miss him. I am alone, but not lonely. I have always felt God's presence with me."

During that time, a friend said to her, "I'm glad you can smile."

"Well, I spent time crying, but I was glad I could smile too." Jeanne smiles, and joy radiates out from her.

"One key to combating loneliness is to keep busy and don't sit around home alone," she advises.

Peace, hope, and joy are all connected for Jeanne. As she contemplates the lives of others, she realizes how God has blessed her. She thanks Him for getting her through every night and every new day.

A poem attributed to Mother Teresa sits on Jeanne's kitchen counter. It's a philosophy Jeanne tries to live by:

> People are often unreasonable, irrational, and self-centered. Forgive them anyway.
>
> If you are kind, people may accuse you of selfish, ulterior motives. Be kind anyway.
>
> If you are successful, you will win some unfaithful friends and some genuine enemies. Succeed anyway.
>
> If you are honest and sincere, people may deceive you. Be honest and sincere anyway.
>
> What you spend years creating, others could destroy overnight. Create anyway.
>
> If you find serenity and happiness, some may be jealous. Be happy anyway.
>
> The good you do today will often be forgotten. Do good anyway.
>
> Give the best you have, and it will never be enough. Give your best anyway.
>
> In the final analysis, it is between you and God. It was never between you and them anyway.[7]

"Be anxious for nothing, but in everything by prayer and sup-plication, with thanksgiving, let your requests be made known to God; and the peace of God, which surpasses all understanding, will guard your hearts and minds through Christ Jesus" (Philippians 4:6–7).

"For I have learned in whatever state I am, to be content" (Phi-lippians 4:11).

Meditation Questions

1. God rewarded Job. What does that say about the worth of a season of suffering?
2. Have you looked for restoration, and then seen it in an-other family member? How did you feel about that?
3. What can you learn from Job's encounter with God?
4. Do you believe in second chances? Even from God?
5. Do you wait as eagerly for Jesus to come as He does to come to you?
6. What does celebration look like to you? Can you see hints of eternity in it?

Journal Question

Has God given you a deep, abiding joy in your heart? Did it accompany a great sorrow? Write about how this has affected the way you live your life. How does it affect your relationship with Jesus? How does it affect your relationship with others?

Prayer

"He will not dwell unduly on the days of his life, because God keeps him busy with the joy of his heart" (Ecclesiastes 5:20).

Lord Jesus, thank You for the joy that awaits us at the end of our journeys—whether it's through an earthly situation or a cele-bration in heaven. You hold our lives in Your very loving hands, and that's all we need to know. All blessing and honor and glory belong to You.

AFTERWORD

*And every creature which is in heaven and on the earth
and under the earth and such as are in the sea, and all
that are in them, I heard saying: "Blessing and honor and
glory and power be to Him who sits on the throne, and to
the Lamb, forever and ever!"*
Revelation 5:13

It could be happening this way . . .

He stands gazing over the table. Some place settings gleam with crystal, china, gold, and silver; others with chopsticks and bowls; still others with golden goblets and knives for spearing food next to wooden bowls. At some sections, bowls sit alone. The table customs of His guests vary, but all will be comfortable in His house. He rubs His hands together in anticipation.

His glance catches at place cards. Late in the day, some of the names are yet to be written. The frown shortly turns into a smile. Time on earth is short.

It's not long now till His Father will give the word and He can go get His people—His bride. He can hardly wait!

Maybe in heaven, around the table at the feast prepared for us, with a jubilant Jesus sitting among us, we will delight in telling stories forever—tales of how God lifted us above our circumstances and put joy in our hearts even through the tears of sorrow. Maybe as these narratives are told, another will admit to a changed life because of hearing the gospel while on earth. Then another, and another. What a wonderful time it will be to see the great tapestry that God wove through His people during our earthly sojourns.

This is what we've been doing through Mrs. Job's story—celebrating together what God has been doing in our lives. Showing, right through our second and third chances, that we can believe Him, and our confidence leads to joy. It strengthens us to continue to move forward into all He has for us. He continues to change us to reflect His image.

On earth, we face war constantly. We pick up our armor daily. When the battle commences, we make sure our helmets fit snugly. We know God gives us power, love, and a sound mind. We hold in front of us the shield of faith to stop ugly thoughts presented to us by the Evil One from piercing into our soul, and we wield the sword of the Spirit. We speak God's words with confidence to extinguish all negative words that fly around us like flaming arrows. We stand on the good news of peace to all men and women.

We will not be afraid.

When the Enemy presses, we overcome through the blood of the Lamb, our Savior, Jesus Christ. He rose from the dead triumphant! He means for us to be triumphant as well. There is power in His blood, and it is meant to cover us.

There are angels around us waiting for the command to defend. Let the Enemy be vanquished! "Let God arise, let His enemies be scattered; let those also who hate Him flee before Him. As smoke is driven away . . ." (Psalm 68:1–2).

After the war, great joy and celebration flourish. The heroes are safely home. The future looks rosy and happy. Life can surge forward in peace. Dreaming and creating are once again possible. Relationships are restored. The benevolent King sits on the throne.

Time is short. Jesus the Bridegroom is coming soon. It could be that fast and furious last-minute preparations are going on in heaven for His long-awaited bride. The table is nearly ready.

Is your name on a place card? Make sure of it. Scripture says the only way to heaven is through Jesus. Through His suffering in the garden, where He faced off with the Enemy of our souls. Through His sacrifice for our sins by His death on the cross. Through His resurrection to restore eternal life to us.

We can respond through repentance, a turning away from our sins, and through asking Him to come into our hearts to clean up our lives. He will fashion us into His image and fit us for heaven.

There is no other way to reserve your place at the banquet table.

When I see a sunrise or a sunset with glimmers clearly shining through the clouds, I can't help but think they are escaping sunrays from God's throne room. The brilliance must be magnificent—more than our human eyes can behold. But when our spirits are ready for Jesus's appearing, we will be able to see the Son clearly.

Do you feel an urgency to set things right with people? Do you feel deep down anticipation? An expectancy?

Maybe there is a faint sound of a trumpet. Do you hear it? Are you ready?

"For the Lord Himself will descend from heaven with a shout, with the voice of an archangel, and with the trumpet of God. And the dead in Christ will rise first. Then we who are alive and remain shall be caught up together with them in the clouds to meet the Lord in the air. And thus we shall always be with the Lord" (1 Thessalonians 4:16–17).

ABOUT THE AUTHOR

Linda Jo Reed's goal is simply to encourage people. Her hope is that support and help can be found through her words. She is the author of *Upheld in the Battle*, a book that shares many of God's gifts of courage, compassion, honor, generosity, hopes, dreams, and more. She believes His intimate passion for His children can be an everyday experience as He is tried and found faithful. Her blog can be found on her website: www.lindajoreed.com. She lives in the Pacific Northwest, is grandmother to nine boys, and is owned by two cats.

ENDNOTES

Chapter One

1. Rod Cosgrove, "To the Ends of the Earth: The ACTS of the Disciple-Making Church" (sermon, Garland Alliance Church, Spokane, WA, May 22, 2016).
2. Seth Godin, "Transitions," *Seth's Blog*, (May 25, 2016), https://seths.blog/2016/05/transitions/
3. Cosgrove, "To The Ends of the Earth."
4. Dan B. Allender, *The Healing Path* (Colorado Springs: WaterBrook Press, 1999), 88.

Chapter Two

1. Taken from *[Jesus Calling, Enjoying Peace in His Presence]* by [Sarah Young] Copyright © [2004] by [Sarah Young]. Use by permission of Zondervan, 56, www.zondervan.com
2. Jonny Diaz, "Breathe," © 2015 Centricity Music Publishing (ASCAP) / So Essential Tunes & Not Just Another Song (SESAC) / Wordspring Music, LLC & Tony Wood Songs (SESAC).
3. Xochitl Dixon, "From Wailing to Worship," *Our Daily Bread*, © 2019 by Our Daily Bread Ministries, Grand Rapids, MI. Reprinted by permission. All rights reserved. March 20, 2019.

4. Taken from *My Utmost for His Highest®* by Oswald Chambers, edited by James Reimann, © 1992 by Oswald Chambers Publications Assn., Ltd., and used by permission of Discovery House, Grand Rapids MI 4950l. All rights reserved, 90.

Chapter Three

1. Ibid, 44.
2. Ibid, 2.
3. David Jeremiah, "Understanding the Difference between Righteous and Sinful Anger," *David Jeremiah Blog*, (March 16, 2012), https://davidjeremiah.blog/understanding-the-difference-between-righteous-and-sinful-anger/
4. Ibid
5. Ibid
6. Marilyn Meberg, *I'd Rather Be Laughing: Finding Cheer in Every Circumstance* (Nashville: Word Publishing, 1998), 125.
7. Taken from *Grace: More Than We Deserve, Greater Than We Imagine*, by Max Lucado, Copyright © 2012 by Max Lucado. Used by permission of Thomas Nelson, 61, www.thomasnelson.com
8. B. J. Hoff, *Thorns & Thrones: Encouraging Words for Faithful Living* (Anderson, IN: Warner Press, Inc., 1991), March 22, 1991.

Chapter Four

1. Mark Vroegop, *Dark Clouds, Deep Mercy: Discovering the Grace of Lament* (Wheaton, IL: Crossway, 2019), 17.
2. Ibid, 18.
3. Ibid, 21.

4. Ibid, 22.

5. Sarah Young, *Jesus Calling: Enjoying Peace in His Presence* (Nashville, TN: Zondervan, 2004), 200.

6. Gail and Gary Justesen, *Better than Before: How to THRIVE in Your Marriage after Betrayal* (Spokane, WA: self-publ., 2013), encouragers2@msn.com

7. Kathleen Hughes, quoted in R. A. Robbins, "The Opportunity to Serve as an Agent of God," *This IS Espirational*, (April 11 2019), https://espirational.com/2019/04/11/the-opportunity-to-serve-as-an-agent-of-god/

8. Susan Wojciechowski, *The Christmas Miracle of Jonathan Toomey* (Somerville, MA: Candlewick Press, 1995). Also, a film by Bill Clark, Formula Films PLC, 2006.

Chapter Five

1. Larnelle Harris and Phill McHugh, *I Miss My Time with You*, © Universal Music Publishing Group, Capitol Christian Music Group, BMG Rights Management, 1987.

2. Frances J. Roberts, *Come Away My Beloved: One-Minute Meditations*, ed. Donna Maltese, (Uhrichsville, OH: Barbour Publishing, Inc., 2008), June 26. Used by permission.

3. Ruth Haley Barton, *Invitation to Solitude and Silence* (Downers Grove, IL: IVP Books, 2010), 16.

4. Luke Dysinger, "Accepting the Embrace of God: The Ancient Art of Lectio Divina," Saint Andrew's Abbey, https://www.saintandrewsabbey.com/Lectio_Divina_s/267.htm

Chapter Six

1. Andy Williams, *Your Hand, Your Heart, Your Love,* 100 Hits Legends, 2009 Demon Music Group Limited.

2. Taken from *My Utmost for His Highest*® by Oswald Chambers, edited by James Reimann, © 1992 by Oswald Chambers Publications Assn., Ltd., and used by permission of Discovery House, Grand Rapids MI 4950l. All rights reserved, 2.

3. Greg Odgen, *Discipleship Essentials: A Guide to Building Your Life in Christ*, expanded ed. (Downers Grove, IL: InterVarsity Press, 2007), 133.

4. Ibid, 133.

5. Ibid, 133.

6. Taken from *[Joy]* by [Mother Teresa of Calcutta] Copyright © [1995] by [*Women's Devotional Bible 2, New International Version*]. Use by permission of Zondervan, 1309, www.zondervan.com

7. Attributed to Mother Teresa of Calcutta. The version used in this manuscript was found written on the wall in Mother Teresa's home for children in Calcutta. Likely based on Kent M. Keith, "The Paradoxical Commandments" (1968; repr., booklet for student leaders, 2001), http://www.prayerfoundation.org/mother_teresa_do_it_anyway.htm

Order Information

To order additional copies of this book, please visit
www.redemption-press.com.
Also available on Amazon.com and BarnesandNoble.com
or by calling toll-free 1-844-2REDEEM.